D0290656

A CHRISTIAN PRIMER

The Prayer, the Creed, the Commandments

ALBERT CURRY WINN

Westminster/John Knox Press
Louisville, Kentucky

Unless otherwise identified, scripture quotations are from the Revised Standard Version of the Bible (with occasional modification), copyrighted 1946, 1952, © 1971, 1973 by the Division of Christian Education of the National Council of the Churches of Christ in the U.S.A., and are used by permission.

Scripture quotations marked TEV are from the *Good News Bible* (Today's English Version)—New Testament: Copyright © American Bible Society 1966, 1971, 1976.

Book design by Gene Harris

First edition

Published by Westminster/John Knox Press
Louisville, Kentucky

PRINTED IN THE UNITED STATES OF AMERICA

9 8 7 6 5 4 3 2 1

Library of Congress Cataloging-in-Publication Data

Winn, Albert Curry, 1921–
   A Christian primer : the prayer, the creed, the commandments /
Albert Curry Winn. — 1st ed.
        p.   cm.
   Includes bibliographical references.
   ISBN 0-664-25101-3

   1. Lord's prayer. 2. Apostles' Creed. 3. Ten commandments.
4. Presbyterian Church—Doctrines. I. Title.
BV230.W52 1990
230—dc20   89-29555
                                                       CIP

To the faithful congregations

of Richmond Second and North Decatur,

who struggled with me to understand

what the documents of the Christian primer

can mean for us today.

Contents

DISCARDED

Preface

In 1985 I published a series of reflections on the Apostles' Creed under the title *Plain Talk About the Apostles' Creed*. The little booklet was brought out with commendable haste by the Presbyterian Publishing House to meet the needs of women who were engaged that year in a special study of the Creed. The reception of that work has prompted me to revise it and to incorporate it in this larger book, which also contains reflections on the Lord's Prayer and the Ten Commandments.

Although I have attempted to keep abreast of the best scholarship, I have retained an informal style of direct address to the reader. Many will enjoy that, and I hope the more scholarly will pardon it.

A. C. W.

Introduction

When my father went to school over a century ago, the first book he was given was a primer. This little book provided the material on which he developed his skills in reading and writing. More important, it presented him with stories, poems, proverbs, drawings, orations, and quotations from scripture that impressed on him the ideals and values of the society of which he was a part. The primer socialized a little boy into late-nineteenth-century middle-class America. It was a powerful influence on him, and to the end of his life he would quote bits and pieces from the primer to his own children as he felt the occasion demanded. He not only quoted the primer, he lived by its principles and standards.

Is there a Christian primer? Is there a brief collection of time-honored words and documents that can socialize children and new Christians and nominal Christians into the Christian society, that can powerfully impress upon them Christian ideals and values? I believe there is such a primer. It is seldom designated as such. It leads a shadowy existence, its presence largely unrecognized and its potential not utilized.

What is it that most Christians know by heart? What words are so familiar that Christians can recite them in unison, even in a time when memorization is out of fashion? The answers come quickly: the Lord's Prayer, the

Apostles' Creed, and the Ten Commandments.* These three are used so frequently in the liturgy of most churches that regular churchgoers find they have learned them by heart without really trying. Phrases from them provide titles for books, articles, and editorials and mark our common speech.

Indeed, the Prayer, the Creed, and the Commandments may provide the only common body of material to which Christian writers or speakers may refer with some confidence that the reference will be instantly understood. There was a time when the church year and the stained glass windows of cathedrals created a common body of Christian stories that were known even to the illiterate. And there was a time when the faithful reading of scripture, especially among Protestants, made the entire Bible familiar territory. Today it may be that we can count on familiarity with only a very meager body of material, typified by the Commandments, the Prayer, and the Creed.

We can rejoice that this meager body of the familiar contains basic pieces of the Christian tradition. The Reformers faced a basic question of Christian education: What should the children of believers know and understand in order to perpetuate the faith in their generation? The answer they gave is precise: The Apostles' Creed, the Ten Commandments, and the Lord's Prayer. These three constitute the backbone of Luther's Catechism, of Calvin's Catechism, and of the Heidelberg Catechism. If there is a Christian primer, a basic book for beginners that initiates them into the realm of Christian learning and remains important to the end of the road, it consists of these three. It is a sign of health, not sickness, that they are still familiar in the church.

But familiarity does not guarantee understanding. The catechisms are seldom studied today. And if they were, they would not necessarily answer the questions that perplex twentieth-century Christians. Today's young people

---

*The great Orthodox churches of the East are an exception; they use the Nicene Creed, not the Apostles' Creed.

are neither attracted nor inhibited by a heavy negative list of "thou shalt nots." Why do some Christians want their "debts" forgiven, and others their "trespasses"? Some Christians do not say that Christ "descended into hell"; if we do say it, what do we mean by it? Indeed, all three documents presuppose a "three-story universe"—heaven above, hell below, earth in between. How do we deal with them when we presently understand the universe quite differently?

Because these basic, familiar documents of the faith are seldom discussed or explained, the church suffers. Many Christians put their minds into neutral and repeat the words unthinkingly. Others are offended and remain silent. Some leave the church altogether. It is tragic that what should constitute one of the church's major assets, its primer, has become either worthless or a serious liability.

Here, then, are reflections on what is most familiar and most perplexing about the faith. They are based on a lifetime of pondering, preaching, and teaching about the Prayer, the Creed, and the Commandments. They may be useful to the church in several ways. First, they may encourage preachers to do doctrinal preaching from time to time and to deal helpfully with the familiar. Doctrinal sermons need not follow a single pattern; they can be as varied in form and style as any other sermons. But they must deal seriously with a crucial piece of the Christian tradition, try to make it clear in the present context, try to answer questions people may have, and urge that piece of the tradition both on the mind and on the heart. Second, these reflections may provide material for study groups wishing to learn more about the Prayer, or the Creed, or the Commandments, or all three. Third, some may find this material useful for private study and devotional reading. It is presented with the hope that, however it may be used, the result will be an enrichment of the liturgy—that when the time comes to repeat the Commandments or to say the Prayer or to affirm the Creed, it will be a high moment, catching the throat, moistening the eye, warming the heart, and stretching the mind.

Part One

The Lord's Prayer

After this manner therefore pray ye:
Our Father which art in heaven,
Hallowed be thy name.
Thy kingdom come.
Thy will be done
In earth, as it is in heaven.
Give us this day our daily bread.
And forgive us our debts,
As we forgive our debtors.
And lead us not into temptation,
But deliver us from evil:
For thine is the kingdom, and the power,
   and the glory, for ever. Amen.

Matthew 6:9–13, KJV

1

Lord, Teach Us to Pray

Isaiah 62:6–7
Luke 11:5–8

He was praying in a certain place, and when he
ceased, one of his disciples said to him,
"Lord, teach us to pray, as John taught his
disciples."

Luke 11:1

We begin our Christian primer with the Lord's Prayer,
or the "Our Father," as it is often called. The Reformers,
when they wrote their primers in the form of catechisms,
usually went first to the Creed, then to the Commandments, and finally to the Prayer. We begin with the
Prayer, however, because it is probably the most familiar
of the three, used most often in the liturgy. It can be
argued that the Prayer deals with our most fundamental
relationship with God, that praying to God is more basic
than saying what we believe about God or understanding
the commandments of God.

The disciples certainly sensed that prayer was basic and
fundamental in the life of Jesus. They had observed how
he stole away early in the morning to pray, how he spent
whole nights in prayer, how he lifted his eyes to heaven
whenever power was needed. They recognized prayer as
the secret behind Jesus' marvelous teaching, the secret

behind his ready obedience to the will of God. So they said, "Lord, teach us to pray."

In one sense the disciples already knew how to pray, in the way everyone knows how to pray. Prayer is not just a Christian function, it is a human function. Human beings are not just thinking animals or tool-making animals or cooking animals, they are praying animals. Some people pray spasmodically, when great trouble wrings a prayer from unaccustomed lips. Others pray routinely from long habit. Very few never pray at all. But prayer as Jesus prayed, prayer as life's basic attitude, prayer as dominant desire and mortal struggle and unceasing joy, prayer as the deep pedal-note of life, undergirding all the melodies on life's surface—of that the disciples knew they did not know. And they were not ashamed to ask, "Lord, teach us to pray."

Shall we join them in that request, you and I? Surely in one sense we know how to pray, and have prayed, some of us seldom, others frequently. But in another sense we are deeply aware of our ignorance and ineptness. For all our vaunted modern knowledge, our technical know-how, our scientific learning, when it comes to this fundamental matter of praying, Jesus of Nazareth has much to teach us. So we too say, "Lord, teach us to pray."

I

In answer, Jesus does not give us a lecture on methods, a set of inflexible rules, or a daily schedule, but a brief, terse, disarmingly simple model of what prayer is:

When you pray, say:
"Father,
hallowed be thy name.
Thy kingdom come.
Give us each day our daily bread;
and forgive us our sins,
for we ourselves forgive every one who is indebted to us;
and lead us not into temptation."

That is the way Luke records it (11:2–4). Most of us are more familiar with Matthew's version (6:9–13):

> Pray then like this:
> Our Father who art in heaven,
> Hallowed be thy name.
> Thy kingdom come.
> Thy will be done,
>   On earth as it is in heaven.
> Give us this day our daily bread;
> And forgive us our debts,
>   As we also have forgiven our debtors;
> And lead us not into temptation,
>   But deliver us from evil.

Before we go further we must stop and ask a critical question. Do we really have here "the prayer that Jesus taught his disciples"? We know that Jesus never wrote a book, never made a tape recording. He spoke his memorable sayings freely, scattering them like seed, and many fell by the wayside. The sayings we have are those that happened to be remembered and treasured by the early church. The form in which they come to us has been shaped and molded by that church to meet its needs and to answer its problems. We see Jesus, as it were, through the filter of the primitive Christian community.

Some scholars, then, have suggested that the prayer as we know it does not go directly back to Jesus, but that the early church took some of his scattered sayings on prayer and wove them into what we now know as "the Lord's Prayer."

According to another point of view, Jesus himself may have deliberately shaped and taught this prayer. We know that in Jesus' day various religious groups had their own forms of prayer. The special prayer, taught by the teacher, unified and identified the students, or disciples. Thus John the Baptist had taught a special prayer to his disciples (Luke 11:1). And when Jesus' disciples requested something similar, Jesus responded with great care. He formed and shaped the prayer in a way in which it could be easily

memorized. In these few words he summed up all he had
to say about prayer, and his disciples seem to have faith-
fully transmitted it. The debates and developing theology
of the early church are not reflected in it at all. It breathes
the pure air of the profound Jewish piety and arresting
originality of Jesus himself.

The biblical critic E. F. Scott reminds us of how Christians in the Middle Ages eagerly sought for some tangible
relic of Jesus: a fragment of his robe, a cup he had drunk
from, a splinter of the cross on which he died. Even in our
own day there has been much speculation and excitement
over the Veil of Turin, the supposed handkerchief of
Veronica with which Jesus wiped his face. But, says Scott,
"In the Lord's Prayer we actually possess such a relic. And
by means of it we touch what was inmost in the person of
Jesus."[1]

That may be as extreme on one side as attributing the
prayer to the early church is on the other. I believe it is
fair to say this: Although the early church may have had
a hand in the Lord's Prayer, as it had a hand in all parts
of the Gospels, nevertheless in this prayer we are probably
in as close touch with the mind and heart of Jesus of
Nazareth as we shall ever be in this life.

II

The very familiarity of the prayer is a problem. I do not
say that familiarity in this case breeds contempt; it simply
throws our minds into neutral gear, so that we do not think
about the words we say. They are so simple that we miss
their profundity and overlook their difficulty. Let us at the
outset observe three simple things about the prayer as a
whole.

In the first place, it is evident that Jesus understood
prayer at its very heart to be making requests to God. Jesus
knew about confession and thanksgiving and all the other
parts of prayer, but his model prayer is basically a series
of petitions.

As if to underline this, the prayer is followed in Luke by

one of the most humorous parables Jesus ever told (11:5–9). It is midnight. The doors are all shut. The man of the house is in bed with all his children. The sweet snoring of deep sleep is the only music. Suddenly there is a terrible racket. The next-door neighbor is pounding on the door. "Get up, get up," he says, "a friend of mine has come on a journey and he is hungry and I have nothing to set before him. Give me three loaves of bread."

"I can't get up. The door is shut. The children are in bed. Go away!"

"Get up, get up, and give me some bread."

"Go away!"

"Get up, get up, my friend is hungry."

"All right, all right! Here is all the bread in the house. Take it, go away, and leave me alone."

Parables usually make one point. And the point here is not that God is a reluctant giver but that we should be persistent askers, not easily discouraged in our asking.

I tell you, says Jesus, ask and ask and ask, and you will receive. Seek and seek and seek, and you will find. Knock and knock and knock, and it will be opened to you.

That's prayer.

This raises all kinds of problems for us. It is hard for us to see how—in a world we picture as regular and orderly and governed by natural law—God will or even can answer our prayers. Moreover, the common human experience is that when we pray the answer usually does not come—at least it does not come in the form we had in mind. In the face of this, a teaching has arisen that sounds very humble, very pious, and very spiritual. It says that prayer cannot be making requests to God. How crude and primitive and magical that would be! Prayer is adjusting ourselves to the way things are. Prayer does not change the world; it changes us. Now this kind of teaching may have a great appeal; it may be what you and I have believed for a long time. But let us be honest: This is not the mind of Jesus about prayer. God invites us to make requests, says Jesus. God shares power with us. God waits for our prayers. There are things God will not say to us or give to us or do through us until we pray. It is this childlike, confident attitude toward prayer that Jesus teaches in the Lord's Prayer. We are going to have to wrestle with that.

III

In the second place, the petitions fall easily into a simple outline. The first three concern God: God's name, God's will, God's kingdom. The second three concern human beings: our bread, our sins, our struggle with evil.

The wedding of these two sets of petitions in a single prayer says something very important. Prayer cannot be confined to lofty, spiritual matters, the name and will and kingdom of God; it must also include common, earthy things like bread and sin and temptation. On the other hand, prayer cannot be purely secular and earthy; it must deal with religious matters as well. Even the order is significant. We rightly begin with God's affairs, because only then can we pray properly about *our* affairs. To fail to put our needs in that larger framework could make prayer a selfish matter indeed.

IV

In the third place, there is another safeguard against selfishness in Jesus' teaching on prayer. In the parable, the neighbor begs bread *for his friend* who has come on a journey. In the prayer, I need bread, but so do all people. So "give *us* this day *our* daily bread." I need forgiveness, but so does everyone else. So "forgive *us our* debts as *we* forgive *our* debtors." I need protection, but we all do. So "lead *us* not into temptation, but deliver *us* from evil." There is an old saying: "You cannot say the Lord's Prayer and say a single *me.*" There is no room here for "God bless me and my wife, my son John and his wife, us four and no more." And that "we," "our," and "us" is not just us Christians but us human beings.

We shall have to wrestle with the implications of those pronouns for racism, nationalism, and special privileges.

Just now I want to point out what those pronouns indicate about the magnificence of prayer. What a magnificent duty and privilege it is to stand before God, not just in our own behalf but in behalf of every man, woman, and child created in God's image; to cry to God for the basic things all human beings need; to take our place among those whom God admits to the inner council chamber and through whose prayers God chooses to rule the world; to be God's remembrancers, charged to remind the Lord of the universe by night and by day of those things God wants to do yet will not do without us! To us are addressed those remarkable words:

> Upon your walls, O Jerusalem,
>   I have set watchmen;
> all the day and all the night
>   they shall never be silent.
> You who put the LORD in remembrance,
>   take no rest,
> and give the LORD no rest
>   until God establishes Jerusalem
>   and makes it a praise in the earth.
>   *Isaiah 62:6–7*

2

Our Father
Who Art in Heaven

Matthew 7:9—11
Romans 8:15
Galatians 4:6

If prayer is more than self-adjustment to the inevitable, the question that confronts us immediately is: To whom are we praying? If we are not just talking to ourselves, or to our collective unconscious, or to the projection of our desires, to whom are we talking?

In the deceptively simple prayer that Jesus taught us, the answer runs thus: We are talking to our Father who is in heaven. This answer needs very careful examination. It contains tremendous truths that do not at first meet the eye. It also presents us with tremendous problems.

I

Among the tremendous truths are God's caring for us and our intimate access to God. Here, as we said earlier, we are in direct touch with Jesus. His unquestioning faith in God's care and availability led him to begin almost every prayer of his that is recorded in the New Testament thus: "Father." He did not invent this name for God. It is found in primitive religions, in Greek and Latin mythology, and in the great world faiths. It is present, although infrequently, in the Hebrew scriptures Jesus knew and loved. However, it is never used there in direct address to God. Jesus' originality was to address God as Father with a naturalness and directness that are unique.

We even know the exact word he used. The earliest copies we have of our four Gospels are in Greek, but Jesus spoke Aramaic, a close cousin of the Hebrew of the Old Testament. Mark, who several times records the actual Aramaic words of Jesus, tells us that in the garden of Gethsemane Jesus prayed, saying, "Abba, Father, all things are possible to thee; remove this cup from me; yet not what I will, but what thou wilt" (Mark 14:36). "Abba, Father"— that's the way Jesus talked to God. And it was an unforgettable memory in the early church. Paul tells us that Christians of the first generation, impelled by the Holy Spirit, began their prayers with the same word, "Abba" (Rom. 8:15; Gal. 4:6).

"Abba" is the family word for God, the word expressing intimacy and caring. Our word "Daddy" is probably too palsy-walsy a translation. But Abba is not a remote, patriarchal, sternly controlling figure. Abba is a child's father: personal, involved, knowing, caring. To Jesus the existence and caring concern of such a God were primal fact, needing no proof or argument.

The Roman emperor approached the gates of the Eternal City in triumphal procession. Suddenly a child darted toward his chariot. The praetorian guards seized the child, crying, "That is the emperor!" "Your emperor," said the child, "but my father!" Just so in complete trust and confidence and familiarity Jesus darted to God. In a day when his contemporaries made God so remote and transcendent that they would not pronounce the sacred Name but used circumlocutions, such as the Power or the Glory, Jesus cried, "Abba, Father," and taught his disciples to do the same. "When we cry, Abba! Father! it is the Spirit itself bearing witness with our spirit that we are children of God" (Rom. 8:15–16).

II

That brings us to the little word "our." Jesus spoke freely of "my Father," but he teaches us to pray *our* Father." God is not your private father. If you are a child in a large family, you learn very quickly that there are some things you cannot ask your father to do. If you were an only child you might ask; but God has no only children.

Here we encounter what has been called the "bounds and boundlessness of prayer." A daughter or son of the Almighty God may well suppose that prayer is boundless. "Ask whatever you will"—so the promises run. But there are bounds, sometimes stated and sometimes implicit. You cannot ask to rise on the bleeding back of a brother or sister. You cannot ask for a personal advantage that will cost one of God's other children dearly. You cannot ask for your nation to prosper at the expense of other nations, or your church at the expense of other churches.

The "our" in "our Father" constitutes us as brothers and sisters who pray for one another as well as for ourselves. There is between us what Don Shriver has called "the bond of tender supremacy."[2] Or, as George Buttrick put it, the pattern of society in trade or politics or the church must become that of a loving family. God is intent on the Beloved Community.[3]

III

Now, straight over the hill come the difficulties.[4] When we begin our prayer with "Our Father," we are in danger of ascribing to God, consciously or unconsciously, a maleness that is not theologically correct, a masculinity that can be oppressive to half the human race.

If you are inclined to feel this is unimportant, splitting fine hairs, I would remind you that in the name of the Fatherhood of God, some of the great teachers of the early church taught that women are defective males and hence less in the image of God than are men. In the name of the Fatherhood of God, some have countenanced and blessed discrimination against women in job opportunities and in pay for the same work. In the name of the Fatherhood of God, women have been denied the full exercise of their gifts in positions of leadership in the church. We simply have to be aware that there are real dangers involved in the inestimable privilege of approaching God as Jesus did. We have to be deeply understanding of feminist theologians who declare that Father has become unusable as a name for God.

There is another side to this argument as well. Diane Tennis, herself a recognized feminist theologian, has written that we must not abandon God the Father. That would surrender to the status quo, would admit that there is no way for the two sexes to live together. It would fail to call unreliable human fathers to reliability. Women, as well as men, need the reliability of a Father God.[5]

It is certainly a mistake to think of God only as Father. The scriptures clearly contain many passages that speak of God in feminine, mothering terms. And those terms are just as effective in conveying God's intimacy and care, and our sisterhood and brotherhood, as are the fathering terms. Pope John Paul I has said clearly that God is Father and moreover Mother.[6] The question is: In adding the Mother language (which we should certainly do, assuring women that they are as much in the image of God as men ever were), should we altogether eliminate the Father language?

IV

We have not solved the complex problems that surround "Our Father," a phrase designed for our deep comfort and high challenge. Perhaps it will help to see if it makes any difference that this Father is "in heaven."

It is true that the biblical writers thought of heaven as "up there." But that does not make heaven the proper object of a space probe. The Bible is more sophisticated than that. Again, if we think of heaven as primarily the place where the blessed dead abide, we need to look once more at our Bibles. Though that idea is not lacking there, the primary meaning of heaven is the seat of God's authority, where God abides and from which God rules. Heaven

is what is not-earth, what is other than the world we know.
To call God "our Father *in heaven*" is to speak of the
otherness of God.

> For my thoughts are not your thoughts,
>   neither are your ways my ways, says the LORD.
> For as the heavens are higher than the earth,
>   so are my ways higher than your ways
>   and my thoughts than your thoughts.
>   *Isaiah 55:8–9*

God's way of being, God's way of knowing, God's way of
loving are not just like ours. They are mysteries to us.

To return to the matter of maleness and femaleness.
Our way of being on earth is to be one or the other. But
because God is "in heaven," God's way of being gathers up
and transcends both masculinity and femininity.

> As a father pities his children,
>   so the LORD pities those who fear him.
>   *Psalm 103:13*

> As one whom his mother comforts,
>   so I will comfort you.
>   *Isaiah 66:13*

So God's fatherhood is not just like human fatherhood.
God is not like the inept, bumbling fathers in the comic
strips or the television sitcoms. Neither is God the tyranni-
cal, patriarchal stereotype: powerful, aggressive, oppressive of women and children. God is certainly not like the
out-of-control fathers who abuse their children, and especially their daughters, physically and sexually. Nor is God
the remote father: autonomous, invulnerable, self-suffi-
cient, isolated, uninvolved. God is Father in God's own
way, a Father who really fathers.

IV

I am sorry to have spent so much time on problems of
language, which may seem insignificant to some readers.
I assure you they are not insignificant. If the language used

in church gives the message to some women that they are less than fully human or that God is more accessible to males than to females, we need to do something about that language.

It may help to see the problem of exclusive vs. inclusive language as part of the larger, perennial problem of all religious language. We have only human words, so we always describe God in human terms; we always use analogies. We know that no analogy is accurate; every analogy contains its own denial. When we say God is like a human creator, we are also saying that God is not like a human creator. When we say God is like a human redeemer, we are also saying that God is not like a human redeemer. When we say God is like a human sustainer, we are also saying God is not like a human sustainer. And when we say God is like a human father, we are also saying God is not like a human father. The same would be true of the mother analogy.

Jesus, it seems to me, goes straight to the heart of it. "What man of you, if his son asks him for bread, will give him a stone? Or if he asks for a fish, will give him a serpent? If you then, who are evil, know how to give good gifts to your children, how much more will your Father who is in heaven give good things to those who ask him!" (Matt. 7:9–11). God is like human fathers, even evil ones; yet "how much more" is God different from any human father!

There is a two-way street here. The imperfect human analogy ascends to heaven, where it is corrected by the only true fatherhood or motherhood, that of God. Then it descends to earth again as a judgment on all the imperfections of our human fatherhood and motherhood. To eliminate the analogy of fatherhood would be to exempt human fatherhood from the judgment and healing that comes back down the two-way street. Again, the same applies to the analogy of motherhood.

Matthew's account offers us some help in our language difficulties. There Jesus says, "Pray then like this." This encourages us to formulate our own individual prayers in the same order, stressing the same petitions but using different language that is sensitive to our situation. In Luke's account, the difficulties of language are more acute. There Jesus says, "When you pray, say." And of course, if we are to say the prayer in unison, it must be in a pre- scribed form. Though attempts have been made to change the traditional form and find one with which all can agree, they have not been notably successful.

Whatever words we use, it comes down to something like this: "God our Parent, both Father and Mother, we are all your children and therefore sisters and brothers of all who wear a human face. You care for us with unfathom- able love, and you judge us according to strictest justice. You thrust us out to grow toward independent maturity, yet you remain present and reliable. We present our prayer to you in confident trust and trembling awe." That is something of what we mean when we say, "Our Father, who art in heaven."

3

Hallowed Be Thy Name

Exodus 3:1–15
John 17

The Lord's Prayer, we have said, is mainly made up of petitions. There are six of them. The last three are for us: *our* bread, *our* debts, *our* temptations. But the first three are for God: *thy* name, *thy* kingdom, *thy* will.

How different that is from our usual way of praying! We rush into God's presence with our own needs and desires and, perhaps, whims and fancies. But when we ask Jesus to teach us to pray, he says something like this: "God is indeed your Abba, your Father in heaven. God knows what you need before you ask. Far more than any human father or mother, God wants to give good things to God's children. But if you would pray aright, if you would exercise that marvelous freedom to ask and receive, you must begin by aligning yourself with God's purposes in the world. You must start by asking and seeking and knocking for God's name, God's kingdom, and God's will."

I

Now the first of these three God-petitions is the most mysterious, because it concerns the *name* of God. What can we possibly mean by the name of God?

If we stop to think about it, the Bible has a great deal to say about the name of God. In our suggested reading from the Old Testament, we hear Moses asking for that name because the people would surely ask him, What is the name of the God who sends you? A little later in Exodus, Moses asks to see God's glory, and God shuts him up in a cleft of the rock and says, "I will make all my goodness pass before you, and will proclaim before you my name" (Ex. 33:19). In the prophets and the psalms there are literally hundreds of references to the name of God. Jesus says in the great high-priestly prayer, "I have manifested thy name to those whom thou gavest me. . . . Holy Father, keep them in thy name, which thou hast given me. . . . While I was with them, I kept them in thy name, which thou hast given me. . . . I made known to them thy name, and I will make it known" (John 17:6, 11–12, 26). In Acts the early Christians rejoiced that they were counted worthy to suffer for the name (5:41).

Yet, as Emil Brunner remarks, in spite of all this biblical material, very few theologians have written about the name of God.[7] And very few of us have a clear conception of what it means. If we can get at God's fatherhood from the analogy of human fatherhood, perhaps we can get at God's name from the analogy of human names. What does it mean that you have a name?

1. It means that you are a subject and not merely an object, a "thou" and not merely an "it." In the modern city we rub against hundreds of people every day whose names we do not know. Even when we try to respect them as fellow human beings, they blend into the general environment. They are part of the traffic, part of the line at the supermarket checkout. We cooperate with them or struggle against them as we do with or against other forces in the environment, like wind and weather. But then we meet someone whose *name* we know, and who knows our name; the whole feel of things is different. We can address such people, and they can address us. We have what Martin Buber calls an I-thou encounter.[8] We become aware of each other's dignity and worth and freedom. The results of the encounter are never predictable. Our schedule, our plans, our whole lives may be changed.

If God has a name, God ceases to be a force in our environment, even the most powerful such force. We no longer understand God after the analogy of the weather, which we have to accept and cooperate with, or struggle against, as the case may be. We understand God after the analogy of another person. Our encounters with God are personal confrontations: our dignity, worth, and freedom encounter God's surpassing dignity, worth, and freedom, and we will never be just the same again.

2. To have a name means to have a secret. Just because these encounters have such unpredictable results, you don't tell everybody your name. Strangers cannot learn your name unless someone who knows you tells them, or unless you tell them yourself. A doctor was telling me recently about new equipment on the neurosurgical ward. The pressure inside each patient's skull can be reported moment by moment at the nurses' desk. It is amazing what medical people can find out about you and learn about you; they can even see inside your head. But there is no instrument yet designed that will tell them your name. You have to tell them yourself.

Just so, there are some things that can be observed and discovered, or at least guessed and conjectured, about God. But if you want to know God's name, if you want to know who God really is, God must tell you. Or at least you must hear it from others to whom God has revealed the divine Name.

3. To have a name is, first, to be an addressable person; second, to have a secret; and, third, to have a story. When you tell a stranger your name, you don't tell very much. But to those who have watched you grow up and have lived with you, the whole story of your life is captured in your name. Your name was given you at birth by your parents. But that name now has a content you have given it by the whole story of your life.

So God's name gets its content from God's story with God's people. In our Old Testament lesson, the Moses story in Exodus 3, God's name gets its content from the fact that God is the God of Israel's fathers and mothers, of Abraham and Sarah, of Isaac and Rebekah, of Jacob and Rachel and Leah. That is what is behind those enigmatic words, "I am that I am." This is not a dodge, but the final truth about God's name. What the story tells us, what God has shown Godself to be to our fathers and mothers, what God revealed Godself to be in Jesus Christ—that is what God is and that is what God will be; that is God's *name.*

II

Now then, *"Hallowed* be thy name." Years ago, when I was on a committee charged to write a contemporary statement of faith, one of my most prized colleagues was a layman who was a self-appointed watchdog for what he called "holy words." If the theologians on the committee were tempted to talk about "regeneration" or "justification" or "sanctification," we faced the wrath of that good man. He would stand up, wave his hands, and say, "That doesn't *mean* anything to me. That's preacher talk. That's one of those holy words." I can see his hands waving right now at the word "hallowed." And it won't help if at this point I say to him, "Hallowed is just a fancy way of saying holy. It means 'May your name be regarded as holy, acknowledged as holy, treated as holy.' " His reply is predictable: "But 'holy' is one of those holy words!"

What does "holy" mean? It means "separate, different, other." "Hallowed be thy name" then means "May God's name be kept separate from all other names. May God's name be treated differently from all other names. May God's name be respected and honored as no other name." We have seen that God's name includes God's *being,* who God is, and God's *story,* God's actions in history. This helps us see two distinct aspects in the hallowing of God's name.

1. The first aspect concerns God's being, the way God is God. We have already touched on this when we talked about "our Father *in heaven."* We said, you may remember, that God's thoughts are not our thoughts, and God's

ways are not our ways, and God's fatherhood is not just like our fatherhood. There is no way we can print "human" in such big letters that it turns into DIVINE. There is no way we can shout "humanity" so loudly that the echo comes back GOD. God's being is separate, different, and other. God, says Leonardo Boff, is the Ineffable, a Word without synonyms, a Light that casts no shadow, a Profundity that has no measured depth.[9]

Is that pretty theoretical? The holiness of God's being may become more vivid to us if we look at some typical human reactions to an encounter with "the Holy." Rudolph Otto explored those reactions in his famous book *The Idea of the Holy.* Let me put them to you in the form of questions.

Have you ever experienced a sense of the *awesomeness* of God? The familiar spiritual goes, "Sometimes it causes me to tremble, tremble, tremble." Have you ever shivered before the Lord? God, says the apostle, dwells in light "unapproachable" (1 Tim. 6:16). Have you ever felt the unapproachableness of God? "Do not come near," said the voice to Moses from the burning bush, "put off your shoes from your feet, for the place on which you are standing is holy ground" (Ex. 3:5). Have you ever found any holy ground in your life?

Have you ever experienced a sense of the *overpoweringness* of God? Abraham said, "Behold, I have taken upon myself to speak to the Lord, I who am but dust and ashes" (Gen. 18:27). Have you ever felt your creatureliness in the presence of God? Isaiah saw the Lord high and lifted up and heard the seraphim cry "Holy, holy, holy," and he cried, "Woe is me! for I am undone" (Isaiah 6:3, 5, KJV). Have you ever felt undone before the holiness of God?

Have you ever experienced a sense of the *energy and urgency* of God? Blaise Pascal, the great French mathematician and philosopher, carried with him always a strange scrap of paper, the record of his encounter with the holiness of God. It was found on his body after he died. It reads thus:

In the year of Grace, 1654,
On Monday, 23rd of November . . .
    From about half past ten in the evening
    until about half past twelve,

FIRE

God of Abraham, God of Isaac, God of Jacob,
    not of the philosophers and scholars.
Certitude. Certitude. Feeling. Joy. Peace.[10]

Our God is a consuming fire. Have you ever felt consumed by God?

Have you ever experienced a silencing sense of the *mystery* of God? Not just that there are some things you don't quite understand, though you are sure a little more study and thought will explain, but a sense that God strikes in upon you from outside the realm of the familiar and the understandable, that God is strange and alien and other. And were you in that instant struck dumb in amazement? "Let all the earth keep silence before the Lord," cries the prophet (Hab. 2:20). And the women fled from the empty tomb "for trembling and astonishment had come upon them; and they said nothing to anyone" (Mark 16:8).

Finally, have you ever experienced a sense of the *fascination* of God? Despite the awesomeness and the overpoweringness and the energy and the mystery of God, have you been intrigued, curious, strongly impelled toward God? "I will turn aside and see this great sight, why the bush is not burnt" (Ex. 3:3).

O God, thou art my God, I seek thee,
    my soul thirsts for thee;
my flesh faints for thee,
    as in a dry and weary land where no water is.
                                                Psalm 63:1

When we experience both the dread that keeps us away from God and the fascination that draws us irresistibly toward God—when we experience that double movement even in the faintest way—we know something of the holiness of God. That holiness is not in our feelings but in God. Our feelings are the shadows cast by the burning light of God's holiness.

In the first instance, then, "Hallowed be thy name" is a petition for the restoration of reverence, a petition that the holiness of God's being—God's "thou-ness," God's secret, the fulness of who God is—may even now be seen and felt and reverenced in the earth.

2. But there is a second aspect in the hallowing of God's name. God's *actions* are holy as well as God's being. "No one is good, but God alone," said Jesus (Mark 10:18). A God who is uniquely and radically good is a holy God. "Thou art of purer eyes than to behold evil," cries the prophet (Hab. 1:13). A God whose actions are pure and unblemished by wrong is a holy God. A God who loves justice and hates iniquity is a holy God. Ethically, God is separate, different, other.

In the Holiness Code of Leviticus 19, God's holiness involves special concern for the poor, the stranger, hired servants, the deaf, the blind, women, the aged. Israel is to be holy as her God is holy (Lev. 19:2). She is to see that the powerless and the dispossessed receive justice—that will be her holiness. Whereas the holiness of God's *being* separates God from God's people, the holiness of God's *actions* is a link with God's people; they are to act the same way. This link with God makes them separate, different, other from the surrounding peoples. They are now a *holy people.*

In the second instance, then, "hallowed be thy name" is a petition that the ethical holiness of God may be demonstrated on earth by the ethical behavior of the people of God; a petition that God's justice and mercy, which are also part of God's *name,* may be incarnate in us; a petition that we who bear God's name may not by our injustice and lack of mercy bring shame and disgrace on it.

III

"Hallowed be thy name."

To begin our prayers this way is to acknowledge that we live in a world where the name of God is not hallowed. It is to call for the restoration of the sacred in a secular world, for the recapture of awe and reverence in a profane world—beginning with our secular, profane selves.

To begin our prayers this way is to reject all idols. No other name deserves our trust, our awe, our final obedience. There is evident kinship between the first petition of the Lord's Prayer and the first three commandments of the Ten Commandments.

To begin our prayers this way is to take God so seriously that we can no longer be serious and desperate about our own importance; we can be humorous about ourselves. How ridiculous we are when we demand reverence for our names, our causes and projects, our reputations!

To begin our prayers this way is to lay the foundation for all the petitions that follow and to redeem them from selfishness. We ask for the coming of God's kingdom, for only then will God's name be truly and fully hallowed. We ask for God's will to be done on earth, for by doing the will we hallow the name. We ask for our material needs and those of others, for in the granting of them God's name is hallowed. We ask for God's forgiveness and mutual forgiveness among ourselves, for that hallows God's name. We ask for victory over temptation and evil, for that brings glory to the name of God.

> Holy, holy, holy, Lord God Almighty,
> Heaven and earth are full of thy glory.
> Hallowed be thy name!

4

Thy Kingdom Come

Mark 1:14–15
Luke 6:20–26

If we would pray aright, says Jesus, we must begin by aligning ourselves with the great purposes of God. First, as we said in the preceding chapter, we must pray for a restoration of the dimension of the holy, that God's holy being and God's holy actions may be revered in the earth, "Hallowed be thy name." Then we must pray that the rule of God in human affairs, which does not seem very evident, may be made actual and real and visible, "Thy kingdom come."

This petition, says Leonardo Boff, is the very heart of the Lord's Prayer, for it is the very heart of the intention of Jesus. "It burrows deep into the most profound depth of our anxieties and hopes."[11]

Someone commented that "Hallowed be thy name" is a bit abstract. "Thy kingdom come" is a bit concrete. In fact, it may be entirely too concrete for some of us. If you feel that religion should have nothing to do with politics, I advise you to stay away from this petition. "Kingdom" is an incurably political word. When we pray "Thy kingdom come," we are not praying to be taken out of the political order into some heavenly sphere where no decisions have to be made about how power and money and services ought to be distributed among people. We are praying that God's sovereignty may come to earth and become effective in the political realm and for the political questions that plague us and at times divide us. We are saying, "Take over, God. Rule and overrule in the affairs of people and nations."

Our resistance to this petition may not be just that it is political but that it speaks of the wrong kind of politics. As American Christians, for example, we may have an instinctively negative reaction to the word "kingdom." Our ancestors fought free of that kind of politics, and we cannot rewrite history. Although in these days of satellite television many Americans have betrayed a strong fascination with the pomp and pageantry of British royalty, the proposal to return to a monarchy, even a strictly limited one, is not a live option. It has even been proposed that this petition be amended to read, "Thy federal republic come."

Feminist theologians have deeper objections. There is, of course, a taint of sexism in the word "kingdom." "Rule" would be a better, gender-free translation. But it is more than a matter of words. Based on women's experience, feminist theologians question all expressions of hierarchy, of domination and subjection. They are aware that the notion of God as Ruler has been used to justify the division of humanity into rulers and ruled and the consequent exploitation of the ruled by the rulers.

It is obvious by now that this centrally important petition will require close examination and hard thinking. I believe in the end we will find in it a radical critique of all human rule that exploits people, plus an energizing hope—a hope that leads the exploited to say, "No more!"

I

To get a proper understanding of this petition, we need to go back to the Old Testament. Years ago, my teacher, John Bright, wrote a study of the kingdom of God in the Old Testament that has nourished me ever since. It is entitled simply *The Kingdom of God.* [12] We find the idea of the kingdom of God as early as the exodus, says Bright, when God brings Israel out of slavery and offers at Sinai to be their King if they will be the people, the kingdom of God. Here is a vision that haunts their whole history. When the promised land was taken and the ark found rest at Shiloh, some wanted to believe that the kingdom had come, that the best of all possible worlds was here; but it had not come. When David had conquered their enemies and established Jerusalem as the capital, surely the kingdom had come; but it had not. When Solomon reigned in glory, when Jeroboam II brought prosperity, when Josiah reformed the worship, surely each of these was the kingdom. It took the bitter experience of the destruction of Jerusalem, the demolition of the temple, the exile in Babylon to teach the people of Israel that no earthly political order they ever succeeded in establishing was really the kingdom of God.

In fact, in the time of Jesus there still remained a party of Zealots who thought they could cast off the Roman yoke by force of arms and usher in the kingdom of God. Most of the Jews of Jesus' time fell into two other groups. One was zealous for the law. They believed that if all Israel would keep the law perfectly for two sabbaths, the kingdom would come. The other group had given up all hope of human achievement and was waiting for a final apocalyptic act in which the kingdom of God would come down from heaven, a stone not cut by human hands, and crush all earthly kingdoms in the final denouement of human history.

II

As we turn to the teaching of Jesus, we should not be surprised, against that background, that he never defined the kingdom of God, as though it were an unfamiliar phrase to his hearers. The phrase was on everyone's lips. Everyone was looking for it, Lo here, lo there! (Luke 17:21).

Perhaps the most arresting thing that Jesus said about the kingdom of God was that it was already present. He opened his ministry, according to Mark's Gospel, with the

stirring declaration, "The time is fulfilled, and the kingdom of God is at hand; repent, and believe in the gospel"
(Mark 1:15). If that is not a statement that the kingdom has
already come, it is at the very least a claim that it is standing at the door; it is imminent; it will come at any moment.
Later, in the midst of his ministry, and especially in connection with his struggle with the evil spirits, the unseen,
demonic powers that enslave and distort the human mind,
Jesus made what seems to be an unequivocal claim that
the kingdom has come: "If it is by the finger of God that
I cast out demons, then the kingdom of God has come
upon you" (Luke 11:20). Once again, when the Pharisees
asked him when the kingdom of God was coming, he answered, "The kingdom of God is not coming with signs to
be observed; nor will they say, 'Lo, here it is!' or 'There!'
for behold, the kingdom of God is in the midst of you"
(Luke 17:20–21). There is no way, it seems to me, that that
can be translated "The kingdom of God is within you," as
though it were a nice inner feeling that has no effect on
the way things really are in the world.

But Jesus also clearly looked to the kingdom of God as
future. He spoke of how we should *receive* it when it
comes, as little children (Mark 10:15). He spoke of the
quality of righteousness we will need to have to *enter* it
when it comes, far exceeding the righteousness of the
scribes and Pharisees (Matt. 5:19–20). He urged us to *seek*
it more earnestly than we seek food and clothing: "Seek
first God's kingdom and God's righteousness, and all these
things shall be yours as well" (Matt. 6:33). Above all, he
urged us to *pray* for it: "Thy kingdom come" (Matt. 6:10).

Jesus left us no careful theological discourse in which he
explains this apparent contradiction in his teaching about
the kingdom. Some scholars have tried to solve it by por-
traying the kingdom as wholly future or as totally present.
Jesus thought and taught in pictures, and it seems to me
the key to our problem may lie in his parables. The kingdom of God, he said, is like seed sown in the ground. They
grow silently, we know not how. But one day, there is the
harvest, and we must put in the sickle and reap (Mark

4:26–29). It is like a net, sunk down in the water where we cannot see it. Pull it in and it is full of all kinds of fish (Matt. 13:47). It is like the leaven, yeast, that a woman hid in three measures of flour. You cannot hear it or see it, but the dough rises and it is time to bake (Matt. 13:33).

So the presence of the kingdom is a hidden presence. There is nothing in the morning paper or the evening TV news that would lead you to suspect that it is here at all. What we seek and what we pray for is that what is hidden from all eyes except the eye of faith will become visible, manifest, effective, actual, real; ready to be harvested, ready to be drawn to shore, ready to bake. And—here is the important point—the hidden presence guarantees the eventual manifestation in God's own time. You can no more keep the kingdom of God from coming than you can keep seed from sprouting or bread from rising.

III

If with the eye of faith we are to look for signs of the hidden presence of the kingdom, what are they? If our insistent prayer for the coming of the kingdom will one day be answered, what will the answer look like? Don Shriver suggests that a key passage is Luke 6:20–26.[13] The poor will have the kingdom, and the rich will have only past memories. The hungry will be satisfied and the full will be hungry. Those who weep will laugh and those who laugh will mourn. The kingdom is the Great Reversal. The last will be first and the first will be last (Mark 10:31). Children will be the teachers of adults (Matt. 18:1–4). Servants and slaves will be the great ones (Mark 10:43–45). Tax collectors and harlots go into the kingdom ahead of recognized religious leaders (Matt. 21:31). Those who exalt themselves will be humbled and those who humble themselves will be exalted (Matt. 23:12) Not those who exercised power, but those who served the marginalized—the hungry, the thirsty, the strangers, the sick, the prisoners— will inherit the kingdom (Matt. 25:31–46).

The test of the kingdom, says Leonardo Boff, is the poor.

This is not because they are especially moral, but simply because of who they are, predominantly women and children, victims of abuse, war, hunger, injustice. When their oppression ceases, the kingdom will be here. "The kingdom comes through the poor and in opposition to poverty, which will have no place in it."[14]

It should be evident by now that the kingdom of God does not resemble our earthly political arrangements, where the strong usually dominate the weak; it is the Great Reversal of them. It does not justify domination and hierarchy; it judges them. To pray "Thy kingdom come" is not to bless the status quo but to cry to God for something very different indeed. To pray "Thy kingdom come" is to refuse to give to any earthly political order the ultimate allegiance that belongs only to God; it is to renounce idolatry.

IV

This petition is above all a prayer of great hope. We pray thus because the kingdom *will* come. Here I want to use an analogy that may strike some of you as strange. The true believer in Marxism is entirely sure that the dream of a classless society will be realized in human history on this earth. It may be long delayed, but in the end the Marxist is going to be a winner. Inexorable economic laws, the irresistible march of dialectical materialism, guarantee that victory. So the Marxist can take it. The dictatorship of the proletariat may turn into the dictatorship of Stalin. All the five-year plans may fail to achieve their goals. The Great Leap Forward may turn out to be a great slide backward. Solzhenitzin may publish the terrible truth. The devout Marxists remain unperturbed. They can wait. They can go to jail. They can die without seeing their dream realized. Because they believe the outcome is utterly certain, they dare to live in ways appropriate to that hope.

It is not difficult to see that this is a sort of secular shadow of the way in which Christian hope ought to work. Shame on us if Marxists live more appropriately to the hope of a classless society than we do to the hope of the kingdom of God! Shame on us if they have greater faith in dialectical materialism than we have in divine providence! It is the followers of Jesus who should have inexhaustible patience and unfailing courage, because we know the kingdom will come.

We should be willing to live by Jesus' demanding ethic, which is not appropriate to the world we live in but utterly appropriate to the world we hope for. We should pray night and day "Thy kingdom come," because this is one petition where all those promises about expecting the answer are definitely true. The kingdom is already here, and in God's time it will come in the fullness of its power and glory.

5

Thy Will Be Done on Earth as It Is in Heaven

Psalm 40
Matthew 26:36–46

The greatest treasure the astronauts brought back with them from the moon was not the moon rocks but a new vision of the earth. Imagine with me that you and I are on the moon. Out of the cold, black, death-dealing darkness of space there rises into view a great, bright, blue ball. There it is: earth, the only place where human beings can live without their space suits; earth, equipped with air and water and all the vital life-support systems; earth, the one self-sustaining spaceship, speeding through the darkness, beckoning us out of death to life. If we cannot successfully get back there, we are doomed. If it is blown to bits while we are gone, there is no other haven. If it is spared and we get back, we shall be home.

Isn't it amazing? Just when all the juice is gone from words that are squeezed dry by familiarity, just when a petition like "Thy will be done on earth as it is in heaven" has become dead and meaningless—this happens. And suddenly it is so new we are not sure we ever heard it before: "Thy will be done on *earth* as it is in heaven!"

I

What is the will of God? All too often we use the expression "It is God's will" when we are forced to accept things we don't like, when we confront the unexpected and the unwanted, when we face tragedy. Jack Spong says, "God is blamed for so much!"[15]

Jesus dared to say that some things are *not* the will of God. "So it is not the will of my Father who is in heaven that one of these little ones should perish" (Matt. 18:14). The writer of 2 Peter understood Jesus well, I believe, when he said that God does not will "that any should perish, but that all should reach repentance" (2 Peter 3:9).

If God does *not* will the destruction of little children, or indeed the destruction of any of us, what does God will? God wills *life.* "I have come down from heaven," says Jesus, "not to do my own will, but the will of the one who sent me; and this is the will of the one who sent me, that I should not lose even one of all those given me, but should raise them up at the last day. For this is the will of my Father, that every one who sees the Son and believes in him should have eternal life" (John 6:38–39, modified). God wills the coming of the *kingdom.* This, as we have seen, was the burden of Jesus' message as recorded in the first three Gospels. The relation between "Thy kingdom come" and "Thy will be done" is very close. God wills *unity,* the overcoming of all that divides and creates enmity and hostility. "For [God] has made known to us in all wisdom and insight the mystery of his will, according to his purpose which he set forth in Christ as a plan for the fulness of time, to unite all things in him, things in heaven and things on earth" (Eph. 1:9–10).

The author of 1 Timothy is surely in line with the mind of Jesus when he writes that it is God's desire for all people "to be saved and to come to the knowledge of truth" (1 Tim. 2:4). *Salvation* is the will of God. How sadly cheapened that great word has become! It means rescue, safety, healing, wholeness, peace, release, reconciliation. When the singer of Psalm 40 tells of being heard by God, being drawn up from the desolate pit, of feet set on a rock, steps made secure, of being taught to sing again, of deliverance, he is describing salvation, and he uses the word more than once. These things are the will of God; they are God's "good pleasure," what God delights to do and to have done.

II

In the prayer he taught his disciples, Jesus affirms that the will of God is done in heaven. In fact, that is what heaven is: the realm wherever situated where the will of God gets done: promptly, without delay; perfectly, without exception; willingly, without resistance. Milton describes it in matchless poetry:

> Thousands at his bidding speed
> And post o'er Land and Ocean without rest.[16]

We live not in heaven but on earth. And how is the will of God done here? The answer must be:

Not promptly: in all the aeons of earth's history the day of salvation, of rescue, safety, healing, wholeness, peace, release, reconciliation, has not yet arrived.

Not perfectly: only in bits of healing, broken signs of wholeness, moments of peace, the foretaste of the kingdom, but not its fullness.

Not willingly: resisted step by step and inch by inch.

For this earth is a network of contesting wills. There is God's will, but also our wills. And our wills are sometimes in contest with God's. We do not usually notice it when our wills and God's will coincide, when God in amazing patience lets our wills be done. We notice it when there is conflict between our wills and God's will. This is why in our usual parlance "the will of God" is something we don't want, something we sadly submit to. And overarching our wills, with a power that seems greater and more cunning than the sum of them, is a mysterious will that our fathers and mothers called the Evil One.

So Spaceship Earth goes its way with a mutinous, bickering crew. Twenty percent have stashed away in their compartments 80 percent of the goodies on board and live so recklessly that they threaten to foul up all the indispensable life-support systems. The other 80 percent live at or below poverty level, without adequate health care, unable to enjoy much or learn much on the trip. It is known that some of the passengers were not well searched before they came on board and have hidden in their luggage weapons that could wreck the whole ship. The crew keeps multiplying at an unprecedented rate, so things are crowded and all the problems become more irritating.

This does not mean that earth has been wrested from God's control. God so designed the ship that this could happen. And in amazing patience and meekness, God permits it to go on this way—an open struggle between God's will and other contrasting wills. The providence of God, says the Westminster Confession of Faith (6.027), extends even to sins, "and that not by a bare permission, but such as hath joined with it a most wise and powerful bounding, and otherwise ordering and governing of them . . . to [God's] own holy ends."[17] "A Declaration of Faith" puts it more simply: "There is no event from which God is absent and God's ultimate purpose in all events is just and loving."[18] God is still Captain of the ship. We are not speeding through space out of God's control and out of God's care. "If I make my bed in Sheol"—hell—"thou art there!" (Psalm 139:8).

There is an element of resignation in this petition. It signifies our acceptance of those things that God permits and yet bounds, orders, and governs to holy ends that we cannot see or understand. But that is not the main thrust. As we said in chapter 2, prayer is more than self-adjustment to the way things are; it is a cry for things to change, for the great positive will of God that is summarized in the great word "salvation" to be done—and to be done here on earth as it is done in heaven. God is interested in earth. God is interested in changing earth and making it like heaven. That, to echo Luther, is God's *proper* will, and that is what we pray for.

In a memorable sermon, George Buttrick summarized the import of this prayer. Thy will be done *to* me—that's the note of resignation. Thy will be done *through* me—

that's enlistment for service. Thy will be done *for* me and
all others—that's the note of joyous anticipation that God
will one day achieve God's gracious, proper will for us
all.[19]

III

We began our study with the request of the disciples:
"Lord, teach us to pray." It seems to me that one of the
central lessons about prayer is to be learned just here.

How do we begin to pray that God's will be done on
earth? Someone asked Gypsy Smith, the well-known evangelist of a bygone generation, how to begin to pray for a
revival. "That's easy," said Gypsy Smith. "Just draw a circle on the ground. Step inside it. Then say, 'Lord, send a
revival in this circle.'"

So praying for the will of God to be done on earth gets
right down to the struggle, the contest, the conflict between your will and God's. You will not learn to pray by
beginning piously, and vaguely and resignedly, "Thy will
be done." The first question is, What is *your* will? What do
you want? How often Jesus asked those who came clamor-
ing and crying to him, "What do you want?" An embar-
rassing question! It is not easy to clarify, to articulate, to
specify what we really want. The very process is instruc-
tive.

Now then: ask, seek, knock, batter on the gates of
heaven for what you want, and look for the answer. Does
it not come? Keep knocking and do not quickly grow
weary. Remember the man who wanted bread at midnight. Does it still not come? Then maybe your will is not
in line with the proper will of God, God's great desire to
bring safety and health and wholeness and peace and release and reconciliation to all people. Maybe what you
want needs correction. Now you are really beginning to
learn in the school of prayer. Now you are ready to pray
with real meaning, "Lord, teach me thy will. Lord, thy will
be done!"

Most of us want luxury and comfort for ourselves. When I think about it, what puzzles me is not that our wants are sometimes denied but that they are so often supplied. Can I really pray for comfort and luxury on Spaceship Earth? The granting of that prayer means that the gap between rich nations and poor nations, and between rich and poor in our own nation, will of necessity widen. And as that gap widens and widens, the eruption of the vast oppressed majority against the comfortable, luxurious minority becomes more and more inevitable. What do you want? And is what you want in conflict with the will of God for Spaceship Earth? Are you willing to pray "Thy will be done," even if that demands a radical simplification of your life so that others, too, may live on earth?

In a deep mystery we shall never fully fathom, Jesus himself learned obedience through suffering. Jesus himself attended the school of prayer. What he wanted that night in Gethsemane was legitimate enough. He wanted rescue, deliverance, safety, wholeness, peace, life—all things that ordinarily are the proper will of God. He wanted to be spared unconscionable suffering—not only the disgrace of condemnation as a criminal, the lash, the nails, the thirst, the bleeding, the dying, but the weight of your sins and mine, separating him from the Father. "Father, if it be possible, let this cup pass from me." No answer. "Then, Father, thy will be done." I have said all along that in the Lord's Prayer we are in touch with the very mind of Jesus. This petition is stained with his sweat and blood.

But when he rose from his knees, he was the calmest person in the garden. And in the next hours he was in control, not his captors. He was the judge, not Pilate. He moved resolutely to his cross in the confidence of a person perfectly within the will of God.

It is through such victories that God's will gets done on earth as it is in heaven. We need lots of them. Fast. The earth, our home, is in deadly peril. Are you open to that kind of struggle and victory in your own life? It will cost you drops of bloody sweat to pray this petition. But beyond your Gethsemane lies that quiet confidence that is beyond all price. Beyond your Gethsemane lies the healing and salvation of all the crew of Spaceship Earth. Beyond your Gethsemane lies a power in prayer beyond your imagining. Come, brothers and sisters, let us pray, really pray: "Thy will be done on earth as it is in heaven."

6

Give Us This Day
Our Daily Bread

Exodus 16
Matthew 6:25–34

We are now at a turning point in the Lord's Prayer. Thus far we have been getting our hearts and minds and wills in line with the great purposes of God. Most children learn how to make a magnet out of an ordinary nail. If you repeatedly stroke the nail in a single direction with a magnet, the inner forces in the nail will get lined up and straightened out and the nail will for a short time become a little magnet, with its own power to draw and attract. So, when we get our wills aligned with the great purposes of God, we begin to pray aright and to have power in prayer.

We turn at this point from our concern with God's affairs—God's name, God's kingdom, God's will—to God's concern with our affairs—our bread, our sins, our temptations. As Leonardo Boff remarks, "Human beings are not here on earth just for God, but also for themselves. God wants it that way."[20] The lesson is clear: Though we should begin with God's great purposes, we should not end there. The Father expects us and invites us to move on to our own needs—human needs, needs of the most ordinary sort. The simple gospel song is theologically correct:

> What a Friend we have in Jesus,
> All our sins and griefs to bear!
> What a privilege to carry
> Everything to God in prayer![21]

I

When we ask God to be concerned with our affairs, the first thing we say is, "Give us this day our daily bread." Almost every word in this petition is worth pondering. We begin with the action word, the verb "give."

Back in chapter 2, looking at the Lord's Prayer as a whole, we noted that it is made up of petitions, of requests, of askings. That may not have jarred us as long as we were asking for God's concerns, but this petition is asking in the baldest form for *our* concerns: "God, there is something we want you to *give* us!" Some people do not like this. It seems unspiritual, ignoble, downright selfish.

The real problem may be that, though we say the word "give," what we really want to say is trade, exchange, or swap. "O God, I am very pious. Will you trade me your bread in exchange for my piety?" "O, God, I am very decent. Will you swap me some bread for my decency?" "O God, I am trying to be obedient. Will you pay off in bread?" This way, bread is not a gift at all. We deserve it. We have earned it. We claim it as a right.

Now the question of rights and deserts and payments is important in human relationships—except in the most intimate and loving relationships. Gifts, not rights, are the language of love. It is hard to conceive of a courtship in which there are not gifts. And any idea of rights or payment would absolutely destroy the courtship. Parents give to children, and children in their own way give to parents. Children instantly discern that the meaning of gifts is not their cost or their usefulness but the love they express. And children also know when the gift expresses, not love, but the parents' love for themselves or their desire to control the child. When a gift is made conditional on goodness or achievement, the message is: I won't love you unless you are good or unless you achieve.

Jesus wants our relationship with our Parent in heaven to be intimate and loving. All questions of rights and deserts are out of bounds. Our Parent does not make love conditional by withholding gifts until we are good. God makes the sun rise on the evil and the good and sends rain on the just and the unjust. God feeds the birds of the air and clothes the grass of the field. How much more will God's own children be clothed and fed? If we, being evil, know how to give good gifts to our children, how much more will our Parent in heaven give good things to us when we ask for them?

To say, as many do, that we need to discard immature, selfish prayer, which makes requests of God, and ascend to a more mature, unselfish prayer, which simply seeks communion with God, is to miss the point of Jesus' majestic "Give." Real communion between us and neighbors or between us and God depends precisely on giving and receiving. The language of communion is gifts. The ultimate selfishness and immaturity is the refusal to receive, the pride that demands that we trade or swap. If we cannot learn to receive like little children, we cannot enjoy the love of God or the love of our fellow human beings. We cannot be well.

II

Now we move from the verb to the noun. Jesus suggests that the first thing we ask God to give us is *bread*. We all know what bread is. No matter what our race or nationality or gender or age or income or educational level, we all need bread and we will all die without it. What could be plainer than that?

Unfortunately, this seemingly simple petition is complicated by an adjective. An honest translation might read, "Give us this day our [mystery word] bread." The word our familiar texts translate "daily" *(epiousion)* occurs nowhere else in the New Testament, and we can only guess what it means or what word Jesus used in his native Aramaic. Working with possible derivations, scholars have come up with translations like "bread for the day that is," or "bread for the day that is coming," or "necessary bread."

We said earlier that the burden of Jesus' parables and

other sayings was the kingdom of God. Jesus seems to have expected that kingdom at any time. On that basis, many scholars suggest that "[mystery word] bread" means "bread of the kingdom." Jesus often pictured the kingdom in terms of a great banquet, the Messianic feast. So what this petition is really saying is, "Serve the Messianic feast today! Let the kingdom come now!"

While that may be one level of meaning in our petition, I resist the idea that that is the main meaning. In Matthew our petition reads literally, "Give us our [mystery word] bread today!" which would fit in well with the kingdom idea. But in Luke our petition reads literally, "Keep on giving us our [mystery word] bread day by day" which fits much better with the idea of ordinary bread in our ordinary lives.

We are unwise, it seems to me, to let this unknown adjective destroy the plain, ordinary meaning of the noun. There is an extraordinary resistance to letting "bread" mean *bread*, material stuff that can be smelled, tasted, chewed, digested, and on which our physical existence in this present life depends. Jerome spoke of "supersubstantial bread," bread that is something more than substance or material or stuff, some kind of "spiritual" bread. So others have taught that "bread" here is the bread of the sacrament, or it is the Word of God, or anything but plain bread.

There is wisdom, it seems to me, in holding to the old idea of "bread for the present day," or "daily bread," resisting impulses to move bread out of the material realm into the spiritual or out of this present world into the distant future. You have only to read the Gospels to see how many times Jesus gives bread to people, sits at table and receives bread from people, talks about bread in his parables. And it is almost always real, material bread. Humankind does not live by bread alone. But we most assuredly cannot live without plain, honest-to-goodness *bread*.

On that interpretation, note the *simplicity* of this request: bread, not cake. The staff of life, not frills. "There is something simple and spare about Christianity," wrote J. D. Jones in one of the great nineteenth-century discussions of the Lord's Prayer.[22] To pray this prayer could demand of us a radical simplification of life.

Note also the *humility* of this request. It is a confession that despite our vaunted scientific advances, our granaries, deep freezes, and overflowing supermarkets, we are still dependent on God for that which is utterly essential for our survival. Is this really true? Ask any agronomist. Should the sun cease to shine or the rain cease to fall or the seed cease to germinate, all our know-how would be useless. At every harvest time the whole world is only weeks from famine. There really is no such thing as a man or woman of "independent means." You can't eat means. Even if such a person's stocks and bonds and savings accounts were 100 percent safe, which they never are, the failure of sun, rain, and germination would leave him or her with the grim prospect of eating the paper in the safe deposit box. There is ultimate wisdom in the little song by Maltbie Babcock:

> Back of the loaf is the snowy flour,
>   And back of the flour the mill,
> And back of the mill is the wheat and the shower,
>   And the sun and the Father's will.[23]

Now then, just because bread is so utterly material, utterly simple, utterly necessary for survival, it becomes a powerful *symbol* for a whole range of blessings, both material and spiritual, for which we must utterly depend on God. The other levels of meaning suggested in our discussion become legitimate if the material meaning remains basic. Small wonder that bread plays the central role in the central sacrament of our religion, where it is the material vehicle of the profoundest spiritual realities. Small wonder that preaching can be described as "breaking the bread of life." Small wonder that a banquet becomes the symbol of the kingdom. Jesus could utilize the symbolic power of bread to say, "I am the bread of life." So, without negating its blunt materialism, this petition plunges to the spiritual depths: "Give us this day our daily bread."

III

Now to the *dailiness*. I am convinced that in this petition, as in the whole prayer, Jesus evokes the rich Old Testament background he knew so well, in this case the story of the manna in the wilderness. Here are the freed slaves, in a howling wilderness, utterly dependent on God for survival. And God provides bread: a little white round thing left by the dew each morning. The Hebrews called it "What is it?"—that's what manna literally means—and some of them tried to corner the manna market and to hoard manna. But it wouldn't work. No matter how industriously they gathered the stuff, they only had enough for that day. If they tried to save it over, it rotted and spoiled.

God has never promised anybody a year's supply of bread, let alone seventy years' supply. God gives us enough for one day. This is fair enough, because the only day we can possibly live is today. How we distort and twist life when we try to live in the future or in the past! We break and destroy ourselves when we try to bear today the burdens we foresee for tomorrow or the burdens we remember from yesterday. Let the day's evil suffice for that day, says Jesus. We are promised strength to bear that much and food to survive that long. Of course we make plans and look ahead. But we pray for one day's strength at a time. And the prayer is answered day after day after day.

We can't get a year's supply of the Bread of Life either. Some of us try to live on the strength of a conversion twenty years ago or of a good book we read last year. These things won't keep. The gospel is not just for the unconverted. The church needs to hear the gospel every Sunday, just to make it until the next Sunday. We are all of us daily pensioners at the Lord's table, for the bread that makes physical life possible and for spiritual food as well.

IV

Now for the little words we skip over so easily: Give *us* this day *our* daily bread. These little words add tremendous ethical and theological depth to what may have seemed thus far a rather simple petition. A statement often attributed to D. T. Niles runs this way: "Bread for myself is an economic problem, but bread for my brothers and sisters is a theological problem."

In using the "us" and "our" we are acknowledging that our supply of bread depends not only on God, as we said earlier, but also on our fellow human beings. How many people, in how many lands, whose names you will never know, worked to stock the shelves of your supermarket? In no way is it "my" bread. It is "our" bread, belonging to the human race in its interdependence. A darker question must be raised. How much of our bread is the fruit of oppression? How much of our abundance is wrested from the sufferings of the poor? How much is what Leonardo Boff calls bitter bread, stolen bread?[24]

When we pray that "our" bread may be given to "us," we are acknowledging that human nourishment depends not just on a physical supply of bread but on the physical presence of other human beings as we eat. Bread is communal. It is no accident that sharing bread is the most powerful symbol we know of human solidarity. It is no accident that Jesus appears in the Gospels, and especially in Luke, as the bread sharer, that he is recognized after his resurrection in the act of breaking and blessing and distributing bread.

When we pray that "our" bread may be given to "us," we are acknowledging that bread is a gift to be shared fairly and justly with all our human brothers and sisters. We are praying that all people may have enough to eat. And we obligate ourselves to do something about the shameful and seemingly intractable problem of world hunger in our time. If you were adrift in a lifeboat with only one loaf of bread left, there is not one of you who would not insist that every passenger in the boat get a share. Isn't it incredible that we can feast and sleep comfortably while so many of our fellow passengers on Spaceship Earth live on the edge of starvation and many starve to death every day?

Those who have studied the problem of world hunger tell us that the basic cause is not lack of technical know-how or the inability of the planet to provide for its population. The basic cause is the lack of a political will to do what we already know how to do. This prayer obligates Christians to attack that root cause of hunger. It is sheer hypocrisy for affluent people to pray this prayer and to remain uninvolved in the struggle for justice.

7

Forgive Us Our Debts
as We Forgive Our Debtors

Psalm 51
Matthew 18:21–35

Here we pass from the bread problem to the sin problem. The Lord's Prayer has a way of getting down to bedrock. We cannot survive without bread. But if we are burdened with guilt toward God and toward our fellow human beings, we may not want to survive. Our bread turns to ashes in our mouths. Just as our physical existence depends on food, so our personhood, our essential humanity, depends on relationships with others and ultimately with the transcendent Other. Those relationships are forever being breached, and forgiveness is needed for their healing and restoration.

The phrasing of this petition presents some intriguing variations. The best manuscripts of Matthew indicate what we have observed already, Matthew's preoccupation with the impending final judgment. They read, "Forgive us our debts [in the final judgment] as we forgave [in our lifetime] our debtors." Luke, on the other hand, seems more adapted to the ongoing life of the church in this world: "Forgive us our sins, for we ourselves keep on forgiving every debtor."

I

The first question we need to ask of this petition is: What is it that stands between us and God, between us and our fellow human beings, and threatens to turn our bread to ashes in our mouths? The obvious answer is *sin.*

The Bible is exceedingly rich in its vocabulary for sin. Sin is owing a debt, trespassing on forbidden ground, missing the mark, overstepping limits, straying from the way, falling to the side, setting up a stumbling block, disobeying, rebelling, acting unjustly, acting treacherously, acting profanely, or being twisted, perverse, evil, wicked, worthless, foolish.

A cause of continual confusion is that Christians today do not all use the same vocabulary for sin when they say the Lord's Prayer. Presbyterians and a few others say "debts," while most other Protestants say "trespasses." Why is that? "Trespasses" is the translation in the *Book of Common Prayer* of the Church of England (the Episcopal prayer book), a translation made earlier than the King James Version. The influence of the prayer book has been enormous on the liturgical practice of all English-speaking churches, even those without written liturgies and those with scarcely a nodding acquaintance with Episcopalians; the widespread use of "trespasses" results from this. On the other hand, English-speaking Presbyterians the world over are deeply influenced by the Westminster Assembly, which convened just thirty-two years after the King James version was published. In its catechisms, the Westminster Assembly cites the Lord's Prayer precisely as the King James Version has translated Matthew 6:9–13. Presbyterians have stubbornly persisted in using that form ever since. The difference is not theological but historical.

Many recent liturgies read, "Forgive us our sins, as we forgive those who sin against us." This has the virtue of making it clear that we are not asking forgiveness merely for poor financial management or for trespassing on someone else's property. We are talking about sin in all its breadth and depth.

There is, however, some value in using the metaphor of "debts" for sins. When we speak of sin as a debt, several things happen. One of them is that we remind ourselves that *we are personally responsible* for our sins just as we are personally responsible for a debt we have contracted. We really can't say that our sins are an accident. We really can't blame other people for our sins, because our sins are debts and we are personally responsible for our debts.

Another thing that happens when we use "debts" for sins is that we are reminded that sin jeopardizes our *intimate, personal relationship* with God. When I went away to college, my father said to me, "Son, I hope you will not borrow money from your friends. Nothing destroys friendships like debts." Sin, then, is something more than what the Shorter Catechism describes (Q.14) as "any want of conformity unto, or transgression of, the law of God." We are not dealing merely with objective, written law; we're dealing with the One who made us and cares for us and loves us. Sin is a failure to give that One what is due. It threatens the most intimate and important of all relationships—our friendship with God.

Also, when we use the word "debts," we begin to understand *the relationship between what we owe God and what we owe to other people.* We're all familiar with the fact that a promissory note can be transferred and you can owe that debt to someone else. In a remarkable way, the Lord has transferred the debt we owe to God to the thirsty, the hungry, the naked, the stranger, the sick, the prisoner: "As you did it to one of the least of these . . . you did it to me" (Matt. 25:40). We need not complain that we cannot find God in order to pay what we owe. There are collection windows on every corner.

Finally, when we use the word "debts," we get some understanding of *the weight and hopelessness of our situation.* If sin is breaking a taboo, perhaps we can find the magic formula that lifts the curse. If sin is breaking the law, perhaps we can serve our sentence and be free. But if we are in debt to God and to our brothers and sisters, how shall we pay? Time does us in. The hungry person we did not feed has starved. The naked person we did not clothe has frozen. The sick we did not visit have died. Those debts are unpayable. About the time our children leave home for work or college, we parents get twenty-

twenty vision. We become aware of what we could have done and should have done for them. But they are grown and gone. The debt is unpayable. Even if beginning at this moment we could perfectly give to God the honor due to God's name by ministering to God's unfortunate children, even if from now on we left undone nothing we ought to do and did nothing we ought not to do, we would not accumulate any moral capital that we could apply to our past debts. We have no surplus, no savings account, no treasury of merit. We are in a hopeless case. And that brings us to the second question we need to ask this text.

II

If this matter of debt stands between us and God, what shall we ask God to do? The answer, of course, is to forgive us. That, says Leonardo Boff, is "the cry of hopelessly sinful humankind directed to the Father of infinite mercy."[25]

To forgive is not to condone. To forgive is not to say sin is unimportant, minor, nonexistent. To forgive is not to pat us on the head and say, "There, there, what you did wasn't really all that bad; it's all right; forget it; don't worry about it." To *condone* sin would be to confuse justice and injustice, right and wrong, to destroy the moral fabric of the universe. To *forgive* sin is to establish justice and then to transcend justice with mercy.

What happens when one is forgiven can be simply stated this way. The debtor doesn't pay the debt because he or she can't. And the creditor bears the cost because the creditor, out of love for the debtor, is willing to bear it. The past is not denied or ignored, but the future is opened in spite of the past. God absorbs the cost of our sins and says to us, "This is real, but it shall not stand between us. I will not have revenge on you. I will not exact payment. I will cancel it. Now let us go on together as before."

Forgiveness is not what Bonhoeffer called "cheap grace." It is very costly grace. If you want to get some idea of the cost, come with me to a skull-shaped hill just outside Jerusalem where three crosses are reared against the black sky. "You know that you were ransomed . . ., not with perishable things such as silver or gold, but with the precious blood of Christ, like that of a lamb without blemish or spot" (1 Peter 1:18–19). As "A Declaration of Faith" puts it, "In the death of Jesus on the cross God achieved and demonstrated once for all the costly forgiveness of our sins."[26]

To pray for forgiveness is to pray for the cross. We would not dare pray so awful a prayer if Jesus had not commanded it. Our assurance that it will be heard rests likewise in Jesus, whose whole life was marked by the forgiveness of sinners, who personifies and embodies the forgiveness of God.

III

We must now explore the link between the divine forgiveness and our forgiveness of one another. The text demands this, does it not? "Forgive us our debts, as we forgive our debtors." That there is such a link is emphasized again and again in Jesus' teaching. Immediately following the prayer, in Matthew 6:14–15, Jesus says, "For if you forgive [others] their trespasses, your heavenly Father also will forgive you; but if you do not forgive [others] their trespasses, neither will your Father forgive your trespasses." Earlier in the Sermon on the Mount he had said, "Blessed are the merciful, for they shall obtain mercy." Luke has a similar saying: "Forgive and you will be forgiven" (Luke 6:37).

The problem with all these sayings is that they sound suspiciously like a quid pro quo, a simple trade-off where we win God's forgiveness by being forgiving. Does Jesus really mean that for every five dollars' worth of injury for which we forgive our neighbor, God will forgive us of five dollars' worth of sin? That would not be costly grace, or even grace at all. The whole teaching of Jesus, and the whole conduct of Jesus toward sinners, runs counter to this. But if this is not the meaning of our petition, what else could it possibly mean?

Part of the meaning may be this: *The very fact that human forgiveness exists gives us hope for the divine forgiveness.* Sinful men and women do find it in their hearts on occasion to forgive others. I am humbled at times to see simple folk who have lived whole lives of continual, almost incomprehensible forgiveness toward cruel and unfaithful spouses, or demanding parents, or wayward children. We may paraphrase a familiar saying of Jesus: "If you, being evil, know how to forgive, how much more will your heavenly Father forgive you!" The petition may then mean something like this: "O God, since even we can at times forgive our debtors, we dare to hope that you will forgive us our debts."

Another part of the meaning may be this: *For us to be unforgiving after being forgiven is an enormity, an inhumanity.* Jesus knew how to use hyperbole—exaggeration—in order to shock his hearers into attention. The parable of the unforgiving servant (Matt. 18:23–35) is a case in point. Forgiven a debt of ten million dollars, he imprisons his fellow servant for a debt of twenty dollars. It is incomprehensible, unbelievable. Just so incomprehensible, unbelievable, and shocking it is for us to accept God's forgiveness and refuse to forgive others.

I have come to believe that the most important meaning of our petition is this: *The failure to forgive others blocks and short-circuits the forgiveness of God.* As Don Shriver puts it, "We cannot step into the circle of God's forgiveness without bringing our neighbors with us."[27] In the familiar parable of the prodigal son, the elder brother remains outside the party in the father's house as long as he is unforgiving toward his brother. It is a self-imposed exclusion. The unforgiving heart puts out antibodies that reject the transplant of God's mercy.

It is not that our forgiveness precedes and prompts God's forgiveness. It is the other way around. Jesus states it clearly enough: "But love your enemies, and do good, and lend, expecting nothing in return; and your reward will be great, and you will be [the children] of the Most High; for he is kind to the ungrateful and the selfish. Be merciful, even as your Father is merciful" (Luke 6:35–36). This became even clearer after the cross. While we were yet sinners, God showed his love for us; while we were helpless, Christ died for the ungodly; while we were enemies, we were reconciled (Rom. 5:6–10). "Forbearing one another and . . . forgiving each other . . . as [Christ] has forgiven you, so you also must forgive" (Col. 3:13). "Be kind to one another, tenderhearted, forgiving one another, as God in Christ forgave you. Therefore be imitators of God (Eph. 4:32—5:1).[28]

IV

The applications of our text are obvious, are they not? *Personally,* how forgiving are you? We talk about grace and we sing about grace, but do you live out of grace? Are you gracious toward other people, or do you spend a lot of energy thinking of what they "ought" to do? Do you find it hard to forgive people who don't do what they "ought" to do? Is there a connection between that and your own inability to live in freedom and joy and celebration of the forgiveness and grace of God to you? "Forgive us our debts as we forgive our debtors."

In the church, how forgiving are we? There's something funny about church. Things we'd never take offense at out in the business world or anywhere else, we take offense at in church. Grudges can be nurtured for years. Divisions continue for centuries. How can we be the proclamation of God's forgiveness to the world when we are unforgiving to one another? Don Shriver sees the forgiveness petition as what really constitutes the Christian community.[29] We are the community of those who forgive one another because we have been forgiven! Failure to be that is failure to be the church at all. "Forgive us our debts as we forgive our debtors."

In the nation, how forgiving are we? The backwash of a civil war fought over a century ago still haunts us. Divisions over the Vietnam War remain acute and destructive. The hawks cannot forgive the doves, the doves cannot forgive the hawks, and caught in the middle are the Vietnam veterans. Policy toward other nations based on revenge is applauded in the polls. A policy based on forgiveness is often judged political suicide, though policies of forgiveness toward Germany and Japan have proven their worth. "Forgive us our debts as we forgive our debtors."

What a time to pray the Lord's Prayer! What a time to stand before God in our own behalf, and in behalf of the church and of our nation and of the whole world, and to cry, "Forgive us our debts as we forgive our debtors!"

8

Lead Us Not Into Temptation, but Deliver Us from Evil

Genesis 22:1–14
Luke 22:39–46

She sat in a huddled heap on the ground, not daring to raise her head: one lone woman, surrounded by vindictive, vengeful men. She had committed a capital offense in a male chauvinist society. She had been caught in the very act of adultery. Moreover, she was a pawn in a struggle between these men and Jesus. They were trying to force him to say that she should be stoned, in accordance with the law of Moses. Jesus simply stooped and wrote with his finger on the ground. Finally he stood. "Let him who is without sin among you be the first to throw a stone at her." Then he stooped and wrote again. One by one the accusers disappeared. Only Jesus and the woman were left. He looked up. "Has no one condemned you?"

"No one, Lord."

"Neither do I condemn you, go, and sin no more (John 8:3–11)."

Christianity is a religion of forgiveness. That is the message of the petition we have just discussed—"Forgive us our debts as we forgive our debtors." But it is also a religion of "go and sin no more." And that is what the final petition of the Lord's Prayer is about: "Lead us not into temptation, but deliver us from evil." Help us, having been forgiven, to wage a stout battle against sin.

We do not receive forgiveness as a sinning license. In W. H. Auden's "for the Time Being," Herod declares that the world is admirably arranged: he likes to sin and God likes to forgive. The final petition of the Lord's Prayer is a bulwark against such a misunderstanding of forgiveness. It is an encouragement to avoid evil, to resist its enticements, to break with it, to seek deliverance from its hold on us.

I

The key to understanding this petition is Jesus' word about "the evil." The last phrase reads literally "but deliver us from *the* evil." We cannot tell whether Jesus meant "the evil one" (masculine), the devil; or "the evil thing" (neuter), the power of evil. But it is clear enough that he meant something quite definite: not just the absence of good, the sort of necessary defect in the best of all possible worlds, but the definite, cunning force that is arrayed against the will of God.

The problem of evil is much greater than just the problem of your sins and mine, though that problem is grave enough, as we saw in the preceding chapter. This world, which God created fair and good, has somehow departed from its Maker, and there is a great rift, a great separation, a great falling away. God's name is not presently hallowed as it should be. God's rule is not presently all-effective as it should be. God's will is not presently done promptly and perfectly and willingly. There is at work in the world another will, an evil will, a will that resists and struggles against the will of God. This will is cunning. It wears a thousand disguises. It seems purposive and intelligent. It is a master organizer, combining our sinful wills into a vast network of evil that seems far greater than the sum of its constituent parts.

The evil makes the world a dangerous place for God's children. It was a dangerous place for Jesus himself, and he encountered the evil—which in the vocabulary of his day he called Satan—again and again: at the beginning of his ministry, at the hour of his death, and all in between. He was "in every respect . . . tempted as we are, yet without sin" (Heb. 4:15).

It is too bad, it seems to me, that the medieval world went to extremes in picturing Satan in human form, with his red union suit, horns, and tail. Demons sat on every rooftop. Ghosts haunted castles. Witches rode broomsticks. Superstition gripped the world and many innocent people were burned, and all life moved under a pall of fear and spells and magic.

It was a good thing when the forces of enlightenment put down superstition, the demons fled, the pall of fear lifted, and scientific investigations and experiments replaced magic. I'm glad I don't sit in my study and throw inkwells at the devil like Martin Luther did.

But behind all the superstition was a reality that the modern world forgot to its peril—the reality of organized, cunning, powerful, and pervasive evil. It operates in the world, no matter what name you give to it.

Isn't it strange that toward the end of the scientific, enlightened twentieth century the whole medieval pack of demons has erupted again as if from underground, and we have astrology, witchcraft, Satan worship, and who knows what else? There seems to be a principle that whenever something is not openly faced and thought through and grappled with, but is rather suppressed and ignored, it will burst out in extreme and distorted forms. After decades of pretending that there is no reality or potency to evil, that it is merely lack of education or the evolutionary lag, we are now witnessing such a regrettable and distorted outburst.

If we had but paid attention to this familiar prayer, which we repeat so often, we would not have forgotten that there are indeed forces outside ourselves that tempt us and entice us to do evil even when we know better; we would not have forgotten that evil can get us so strongly in its grip that only some other force outside ourselves, the love and power of God, can deliver us.

The world is a dangerous place for God's children. It is

perhaps more dangerous now, more in the grip of evil, than ever before. The tares have grown along with the wheat. As we have made progress on many fronts and the world has in some respects become a better place, so has evil progressed. Its symbol is no longer a grotesque figure in a red union suit but an intelligent bomb that can hit many targets at once and kill indiscriminately and poison earth and air and water for the long future.

II

In such a world we are taught to pray, "Lead us not into temptation."

Or, as the West Indian folk version has it, "Leave us not to the devil to be tempted."

Or, as *The New English Bible* suggests, "Do not bring us to the test."

In some ways this is a puzzling petition. Does it imply that God would lead us into temptation, would entice us to do evil? That is not God's role. The Letter of James makes this clear by saying in effect: "Let no one say when tempted, 'I am tempted by God'; for God cannot be tempted with evil, and neither does God tempt anyone; but everyone is tempted when he is drawn away of his own lust and enticed" (James 1:13–14). One helpful suggestion is that in the Aramaic (which Jesus spoke) the expression may have been, "Do not allow us to be led into temptation."

The confusion deepens when we realize that in the original language the same word may mean either "temptation," where the desired outcome is enticement to evil, or "test," where the desired outcome is proof of faithfulness and strengthening of character. God does not tempt, but God does test. God put Abraham to the terrible test of giving up his own son. God put God's own son to the test in the garden of Gethsemane.

Why should we be taught to pray, "Do not bring us to the test"? This dangerous world is full of tests. Is this a way of praying "Stop the world, I want to get off"? Jesus refused to pray such a prayer for his disciples. "I do not pray that thou shouldst take them out of the world, but that thou shouldst keep them from the evil" (John 17:15). As all parents know, as they watch their children leave home, you cannot grow to maturity—physical, mental, or spiritual—except as you are exposed to this dangerous world. It is the only school of character. Every Christian knows that God does put us to the test and that tests, properly endured, strengthen our faith and align our wills to God's will.

> When through fiery trials thy pathway shall lie . . .
> The flame shall not hurt thee; I only design
> Thy dross to consume and thy gold to refine.[30]

We will be put to the test. Why should we pray, "Do not bring us to the test"?

It is, I believe, to keep us from overconfidence in our own strength. There is something in us that wants to say to God, "Put me to the test. I can pass it. Bring on the tempter; I can defeat him in fair combat." Or, as Peter put it, "Even though they all fall away, I will not"; "I am ready to go with you to prison and to death" (Mark 14:29; Luke 22:33). Peter did go as far as the garden, and there he went to sleep. And Jesus warned him: "Pray that you may not enter into temptation" (Luke 22:40, 46). Far better he should have prayed that prayer than have made his boast. For later that night he denied that he ever knew Jesus.

"Truly, I say to you," said Jesus at the Last Supper, "one of you will betray me." And they all said, "Lord, is it I?" (Mark 14:18–19). Didn't they know? No, they did not know. And you and I do not know. There is no one reading these words who is automatically and completely and forever incapable of base denial of Jesus Christ, or of the foulest crimes for which we now despise those whom we call criminals.

> In the hour of trial,
> Jesus, plead for me;
> Lest by base denial

I depart from Thee;
When thou seest me waver,
With a look recall,
Nor for fear or favor
Suffer me to fall.[31]

Lead us not into temptation! Do not bring us to the test
alone, without your help! Do not abandon us in our weakness to the tempter's power!

III

What if we do fall? Even then we are not forever undone. The prayer goes on, "Deliver us from the evil." Evil
is so insidious, cunning, and powerful that we cannot deliver ourselves. But there is a power outside ourselves that
can deliver us, a power more powerful than the evil, the
power of God. The original is very graphic—God can
snatch us from the grasp of the evil.

In the book of Daniel is the story of Shadrach, Meshach,
and Abednego. You remember it. These three Jewish boys
refused to worship the golden image set up by Nebuchad-
nezzar, the king of Babylon. He threatened to cast them
into a fiery furnace unless they obeyed. Their reply was
this: "Our God whom we serve is able to deliver us from
the burning fiery furnace; and he will deliver us out of
your hand, O king. But if not, be it known to you, O king,
that we will not serve your gods or worship the golden
image which you have set up" (Dan. 3:17–18).

There you have it. The world is a dangerous place. And
if we trust ourselves to be strong enough to resist all temptations, to pass all tests in our own strength, we are fools.
But our God is able to deliver us. There is no miry pit of
depression so deep that God cannot draw us out of it.
There is no compulsion to alcohol or other drugs so enslaving that God cannot give us victory over it. There is no
addiction to nuclear weapons so strong that God cannot
enable us to overcome it. There is no distortion of our
highest and best into our lowest and worst so clever that

God cannot reveal it to us and deliver us from it. And God will deliver us. This prayer will be answered. But if not, if beyond our understanding we are burned to a crisp in the furnace of life, we can still trust God, we can still hang on to our integrity in the face of death. That is all the deliverance he granted to his own son. But in that death all the powers of the evil were trumped and defeated. Death itself was overthrown. And there was deliverance not only for himself but for us all.

All the petitions of the Lord's Prayer are now before us. There are three for God: God's name, God's kingdom, God's will. And there are three for all humankind: bread—what we need in order to survive day by day to the end of our appointed days; forgiveness—breaking down the barriers between us and God and our neighbors; deliverance—from the power of evil. Is that really all we need to pray for? There are many details we can bring to God in prayer. Do they all boil down to this? Is it all there?

I look at all the shiny things advertised on TV. They are so much tinsel compared to bread, forgiveness, deliverance. Perhaps I do not really need anything more for myself.

But for my children. I want so much for them. Yet if I pray they may have what they need to survive, and have forgiven and forgiving hearts, and have help in the struggle against evil, is there more that I can rightly ask or confidently expect God to provide?

Then I think of the great mass of humanity, whose names we do not know but in whose behalf we stand before God, and the words come: "Give *us* this day *our* daily bread. And forgive *us our* debts as *we* forgive *our* debtors. And lead *us* not into temptation, but deliver *us* from evil."

It's all there.

And God has promised to answer.

Lord, teach us to pray!

9

Thine Is the Kingdom, the Power, and the Glory Forever

1 Chronicles 29:10–13
Revelation 11:15–19

The majestic ending of the Lord's Prayer, so familiar to all of us, is not part of the prayer as Jesus taught it. Luke shows no acquaintance with it, and the best manuscripts of Matthew omit it. It is an addition made by the early church. It was made very early: by the end of the first century Christians were praying the prayer in a form that is quite similar to the one that is traditional among us today.[32]

Roman Catholic piety bears appropriate testimony to the distinction between this ending and the rest of the prayer. The form prescribed for individual prayer ends with "Lead us not into temptation, but deliver us from evil." But the form prescribed for the assembled church in its liturgy ends with "Thine is the kingdom, and the power, and the glory forever. Amen."

The early church did not invent this closing praise out of thin air. They found it in scripture. It is clearly based on the prayer that the chronicler places in David's mouth as David finishes assembling all the materials for the great temple that Solomon will build: "Blessed art thou, O LORD, the God of Israel our father, for ever and ever. Thine, O LORD, is the greatness, and the power, and the glory, and the victory, and the majesty; for all that is in the heavens and in the earth is thine; thine is the kingdom, O

LORD, and thou art exalted as head above all" (1 Chron. 29:10–11).

Jesus taught this prayer before the triumph of the resurrection. According to Luke, he was on the way to Jerusalem, with the shadow of the cross falling across his face. Appropriately, he ended the prayer on a somber note: "Lead us not into temptation, but deliver us from evil." But the early church, which had experienced the cross and the resurrection and the spread of the gospel under persecution and the glory of martyrdoms, felt compelled to add a note of triumph. Leonardo Boff says that "Lead us not into temptation" is a cry of anguish and "Deliver us from evil" is a final paroxysm.[33] The early church was unwilling to leave it there.

Should we, on the basis of the best manuscripts, knowing that Jesus did not teach this part of the prayer, leave it out when we pray it liturgically? Or should we continue to accept the liturgical practice of the church all the way back to the first century? I would choose to leave it in. Don Shriver says, "Only sheer ingratitude and historical ignorance would impel anyone to ban these words from the contemporary liturgies of the church."[34]

This part of the prayer is not a petition. It is an affirmation. The affirmation corresponds in an interesting way to the first three petitions. We pray "Hallowed be thy name"; and we affirm "Thine is the glory." We pray "Thy kingdom come"; and we affirm "Thine is the kingdom." We pray "Thy will be done"; and we affirm "Thine is the power." We are saying that what we have asked for is present fact, already done. What we pray for is the ultimate truth about the universe. Our prayer has its answer as we make it. This accords with the teaching of Jesus: "Whatever you ask in prayer, believe that you have received it, and it will be yours" (Mark 11:24).

At the heart of biblical faith we do not find a syllogism, an airtight argument sealed with a *therefore*—all's right with the world, therefore let us have faith, therefore let us praise God. At the heart of biblical faith we find a non sequitur, something that does not logically follow at all, sealed with a *nevertheless*. Much is wrong with the world, the mystery of evil is great, nevertheless let us have faith, nevertheless let us praise God.

Herod is king and has slain the innocent children of Bethlehem. Nero is king and has burned Christians as torches for his garden party. In our century the rulers of the nations, including our own, have ordered the death of more children than Herod ever dreamed of, of more Christians than existed in Nero's day. Today's rulers have readied weapons for the destruction of the human race. *Nevertheless,* thine is the kingdom!

Herod has the power to make refugees of the poor. Pilate has the power of capital punishment. In our century there are refugees by the million, and hundreds wait on death row. The powerful grow more powerful and get their will done ruthlessly. The powerless grow weaker and less able to get anything they want. When the church tries to play the power game, it loses its authority. God sides with the powerless and seems weak and foolish. *Nevertheless,* the foolishness of God is wiser than human wisdom and the weakness of God is stronger than human strength (1 Cor. 1:25). *Nevertheless,* thine is the power!

Augustus reigns in glory; so do the rulers of this present age. Crowds cheer the gladiators; in our day the glory belongs to the athletes and the rock singers and the TV comics. God's name is despised and dishonored. *Nevertheless,* thine is the glory!

Does the prayer end with a great self-deception? Are we saying that what is obviously not true is true after all? Not exactly. The Hebrew prophets used a strange and wonderful grammar. They spoke of the certain future in the present tense. What God says will be, already is! The end of our prayer declares that in spite of those who presently exercise the rule and the power and the glory, in spite of the ecological crisis and the nuclear buildup and all else that threatens us, this is the world's future: God's name shall be hallowed, God's kingdom shall come, God's will shall be done! We cannot say how or when, but the promises of God stand sure. So we end our prayer by shouting in the grammar of the prophets, Tomorrow is here! As Don Shriver puts it, "When we add the doxology to the Lord's Prayer, along with the early church, we are leaping ahead, so to speak, to claim our places in the hallelujah chorus of the end-time."[35]

Why do we stand for the "Hallelujah Chorus" when Handel's *Messiah* is performed? Not just because a king of England stood long ago. Because that magnificent text from Revelation declares our wildest hopes to be present truth. And Handel found music that says, "Yes, it is true after all!"

Quiet, now. Can you hear it above the wails of the ambulances, fire engines, and police cars? Above the whine of jets carrying death on their wings, the throbbing of submarines carrying death into the depths of the sea, the crash of falling bombs, the roar of helicopters, the rattle of small arms? Above the strident debates in Congress and in the United Nations? Above the anodyne of rock music that numbs our eardrums to the uglier noises of life? Do you hear it?

> The kingdoms of this world are become
> the kingdoms of our Lord and of his Christ;
> and he shall reign for ever and ever.
> Hallelujah, hallelujah, hallelujah!

To which we say, "Amen!" It is so. May it be so. And may we live now as though it were already so. Amen and amen.

Part Two

The Apostles' Creed

I believe in God the Father Almighty, Maker of heaven and earth,

And in Jesus Christ his only Son our Lord; who was conceived by the Holy Ghost, born of the Virgin Mary, suffered under Pontius Pilate, was crucified, dead, and buried; he descended into hell; the third day he rose again from the dead; he ascended into heaven, and sitteth on the right hand of God the Father Almighty; from thence he shall come to judge the quick and the dead.

I believe in the Holy Ghost; the holy catholic Church; the communion of saints; the forgiveness of sins; the resurrection of the body; and the life everlasting. Amen.

10

I Believe

Mark 9:24
Romans 10:9–10

Why should we study the Apostles' Creed?

In order that our worship may be more intelligent—that's the first reason. In many congregations the Apostles' Creed is used every Sunday as an act of worship. Even those congregations that use a variety of creeds and affirmations of faith come back to it time and again. The danger is that it can become an empty form, a vain repetition, said with the mind in neutral gear.

Most of us know the story of Helen Keller, blind, deaf, and dumb, and of the skillful teacher who brought her into communication with the world in spite of all her handicaps. Little Helen learned many words, which were carefully spelled out into her hand, but she did not understand their meanings, until one day the teacher spelled w-a-t-e-r and then poured water into her hand. It is difficult to describe the drama and the power of that breakthrough, as word and meaning were finally connected in Helen's brain. I covet for all of us a breakthrough of that kind with regard to the words of the Apostles' Creed.

In order that the offense of the creed may be faced—that's the second reason. Christianity is offensive. It is a scandal. It is a stumbling block to the Jews and foolishness to the Greeks. And much of that offensiveness is concentrated in this brief, ancient creed. "Born of the Virgin Mary"—some people find that unbelievable. "Descended into hell"—some churches even omit that phrase. "Ascended into heaven"—what kind of space trip is that? "Holy catholic church"—some Protestants change that. "Resurrection of the body"—that's much more offensive than "immortality of the soul." More than once in my ministry thoughtful people have said to me: "I cannot join the church because as a citizen of the twentieth century I cannot say things like that." I think we need to face and deal with the offense of the creed.

In order that the power of the creed may be experienced—that's the third reason. We know there was power there once upon a time. Men and women and boys and girls died for these phrases. Life itself was not as precious to them as these truths. "The church," says Rachel Henderlite, "is wistful for the unforgettable radiance of the first century, wistful for the full meaning that is undoubtedly contained in the creeds of the church but has been lost from the experience of many church members."[1] Wouldn't it be great if this dusty document would live again among us in pristine power?

So we begin as the creed begins: "I believe." The Latin for "I believe" is *credo,* from which we get the word "creed." What does it mean to say "I believe"? Does it mean "I can prove it—all the evidence points to this"? Or does it mean "I have no evidence at all; I just like to think this way"? Or does it mean "I really don't care; have it your way"? It surely means none of those things, but what does it mean? I propose that we try to unpack the meaning of this phrase by a careful look at two passages in the New Testament.

I

Mark 9:14–29 tells with great vividness the story of one of Jesus' miracles. There was a little boy whose symptoms strongly suggest what we today call epilepsy. The disciples could not heal him. Jesus returned and questioned the boy's father about his son's troubles. The distraught father says: "If you can do anything, have pity on us and help us."

Jesus replies: "If you can! All things are possible to him who believes." The father responds with a loud cry and begins to say over and over again, "I believe; help my unbelief. I believe; help my unbelief."

Believing is passionate. Some of the old manuscripts say the father cried out with tears, and certainly tears were appropriate. There is nothing dispassionate or uninvolved or detached about that kind of believing. The father does not use the phrase so often heard on the floor of presbytery, "I have no zeal in the matter." He is consumed with zeal.

Dr. John A. Mackay, who was president of Princeton Seminary, was a matchless phrasemaker, and his phrase one year was "the balcony and the road." Some people try to be Christian believers on the balcony, up there, detached, dispassionately observing life below. But Christians have to be down on the road, caught in the traffic, jostled by others, amid the cries and sweat and smell of life. Believing is a road matter.

Again, *believing is dynamic.* There is power in it. The healing of the son is related to the believing of the father. It makes a difference. It changes the situation. It lays hold on God's power.

And then, *believing is a struggle.* It coexists with unbelief. "Lord, I believe; help my unbelief." Real believing is always in spite of. We do not say, "Of course I believe." We say, "I dare to believe, in spite of all the evidence to the contrary." Believing, then, is risky. You could be wrong. It is a matter of decision, and not a matter of course.

II

In Romans 10:5–13 the setting is different. There is here no question of a healing or of a desperate human need. The setting is perhaps a church service, where people are confessing their faith. "If you confess with your lips that Jesus is Lord and believe in your heart that God raised him from the dead, you will be saved." True believing, says

Paul, is a matter of both mouth and heart, both inward conviction and outward confession. There is, in short, no real believing that is simply words in which the heart is lacking. And there is no real believing that stops with the heart, sticks in the throat, and refuses to go public.

III

So far so good. But the situations in Mark and Romans are so different that some have even suggested there are two kinds of believing in the New Testament: believing that will work miracles, or at least makes miracles possible, and believing in what we publicly profess in church.

No! They are essentially the same. The point of juxtaposing these two passages is to say that the belief we put into words in our confession, in our creed, is the same kind of heart-belief the agonized father had as he held his epileptic son in his arms.

As that father had to *struggle* with unbelief, so must we. We spoke earlier of the offensiveness of the creed. Kierkegaard says there is no possibility of belief where there is no possibility of offense.[2] If everything is clear and obvious, if there is no threat and no risk, there is no believing. I find no delicate way to say this. We ought to sweat when we say the creed.

As the faith of that father was a *decision*, so is ours. Faith is not believing seven impossible things before breakfast. It is not believing whatever you want to believe on insufficient evidence. On all the real questions of faith, the evidence is mixed. There is considerable evidence that there is no God, but there is also considerable evidence that God lives and reigns. There is considerable evidence that Jesus was a mistaken visionary, a martyred idealist, but there is also considerable evidence that he was and is the son of the living God. As Pascal said long ago, "You must wager."[3] Or as Browning put it, "Like you this Christianity or not? . . . Has it your vote to be so if it can?"[4] "You Bet Your Life" is not just the name of an old TV show; it's what you do every time you say the creed!

As the faith of that father opened the door to God's *power,* so does ours. It is staggering to think how many people might plug into the healing power of God if they really believed in the forgiveness of sins—believed enough to forgive themselves. And to think how many of our physical diseases are rendered powerless to frighten and destroy us by the simple words, "I believe in the resurrection of the body." And to think how oppressive political powers are disarmed by the phrase, "I believe he sitteth on the right hand of God." Whenever a human ruler wishes to become absolutely powerful, that ruler must attack and destroy this creed.

So we ought to say the Apostles' Creed just as passionately as that father cried out long ago, "I believe; help my unbelief." Either the articles of the creed are passionate, dynamic, decisive, risky affirmations, or they are just empty sounds.

Maybe we can summarize this by looking at three words in our exceptionally rich English language. We have talked of believing, and we have talked of faith. In biblical thought, we do not need to make any distinction between the two, as though belief is a matter of the head and faith of the heart. "Believe" is the verb and "faith" is the noun, and they both translate the same root in the original. But there is a third English word that is better than either. It is both a noun and a verb, and I believe it is closer to the original. That word is "trust."

If I ask you, "Do you trust me?" we have skipped all intellectual games and come immediately to the bottom line. I am asking you to put your life in my hands, to wager it all on me, to trust me.

So what the creed is saying is: "I put my trust in God the Father Almighty, Maker of heaven and earth. . . . I put my trust in Jesus Christ his only Son our Lord. . . . I put my trust in the Holy Ghost."

It is a struggle to say those words. It is risky. It does make us sweat. But it is liberating beyond our wildest imaginations. It is healing, physically and mentally. It is saving in the broadest dimensions of the word "salvation": wholeness, health, safety, peace, deliverance, freedom.

"If you confess with your lips that Jesus is Lord, and believe in your heart that God has raised him from the dead, you will be *saved!*"

11

God the Father Almighty, Maker of Heaven and Earth

Malachi 2:10
Galatians 4:4–7

We continue with our study of the Apostles' Creed, and the words before us are: "I believe in God the Father Almighty, Maker of heaven and earth." In the light of the preceding study, the statement means something like this: With risk and passion, and in spite of all the evidence to the contrary, I have decided to put my ultimate trust in God the Father Almighty, Maker of heaven and earth.

God is the vastest subject we human beings can possibly discuss, and the world's libraries are full of thick volumes about God, but this little creed says what is necessary in just eight words: the Father Almighty, Maker of heaven and earth. If we can say those eight words and begin to understand them, we will be wiser than many whose wisdom has dazzled and impressed the world.

I

I believe in God the Father. This is our creed's first word about God, and it is a good word, although it confronts us with severe problems.[5]

If your consciousness has been raised on the matter of inclusive language, you sense immediately that the creed is in deep trouble. Is it usable at all?

There is no evading the fact that "father" is a masculine word. There is no evading the long history of masculine domination in the church. For centuries women have been treated as second-class members, unable to hold office, exercise power, or devote their full talents to the service of God. Males have evoked the name "Father" as the basis for masculine domination, for patriarchy, for centering all power and authority in men.

In understandable rebellion against patriarchy, some feminists have advocated "womanspirit" theology. God is treated as exclusively feminine. All male language and concepts are taboo. This is a separatist religion, with no room for males as worshipers or as objects of worship. It is often nonbiblical, embracing goddesses or a prebiblical Mother Goddess.

Other feminist theologians advocate an androgynous God, who is both feminine and masculine and is best described or addressed as Parent.

Others have argued that parent language won't do, because it keeps us dependent, immature, perpetual children. So we are confined to terms like Creator, Sustainer, Redeemer.

Diane Tennis argues that "parents are too omnipresent and too significant in the experience of humankind to be exorcised from religious imagination and symbols."[6] We need to speak of God as both Father and Mother. When God is spoken of as Father in the Old Testament, and particularly in the familiar address of Jesus to "Abba"— "dear Father"—it is not a symbol of patriarchy, of male domination and violence. It is an image of care, closeness, compassion, love, suffering judgment, forgiveness, reconciliation, new beginnings, intimacy, tenderness, availability, reliability. To abandon the name "Father" for God is to lose the biblical picture of the divine fathering, which is a model for what human fathering ought to be and a necessary comfort to men and women alike.

If Tennis is right, I believe we can continue to use the creed with two provisos: provided that we keep constantly in mind the rich biblical imagery of the motherhood of God; and provided that we understand the fatherhood of God as distinct from patriarchy and, indeed, subversive of it. "I believe in God the Father" means that God cares for us, is really concerned about our troubles and our needs and our joys. It means that God wants us to grow up and take responsibility for our lives, sometimes leaving us alone in our pain and perplexity so we can grow. It means God judges us and disapproves of all that is sinful and wrong in us and works to correct us. It means God loves not indulgently but wisely, drawing out the best in us. It means God teaches us. It means God suffers for and with us. Even God's wrath means that God cannot ignore us and let us destroy ourselves in a detached and uncaring way. God's love for us is always a just love. And God's justice toward us is always loving justice.

Now, God's love is not immediately evident, not at all. There is evidence for it, but there is much evidence against it. As I walk the hospital corridors, and as I come to know more and more the tensions and agonies of people's lives, the question is unavoidable: Would a loving Father let his children suffer so? Why does a loving Father permit incurable illnesses, deaths of loved ones, handicapped children, broken marriages, lost jobs, and so on? If we still believe God is our loving Father, we believe it in spite of contrary evidence, with risk and passion. "Lord, I believe; help my unbelief."

One more word before we leave this subject. God is our Father, because God is the Father of our Lord Jesus Christ. We do not believe God to be Father because of observation of the world in general and the way things go from day to day. We believe God to be Father because, when the time had fully come, God sent forth the Son, born of woman, born under the law, to redeem those who were under the law, so that we might receive adoption as sons and daughters. It is the Spirit of the Son, Jesus Christ, that *cries out* in our hearts—the same word that described the passionate cry of the father of the epileptic boy in Mark

9:24—"Abba, Father." That's what gives us the courage to believe.

II

The next word is "Almighty." We come to speak of God's sovereignty and power. God is almighty as a Father. God's power is not some bare, naked, amoral "power in itself." All those absurd questions—Can God make a weight God cannot lift? Can God lie? and so on—are seen in their absurdity. God is the Father Almighty, the Almighty Father. God has all the power God needs to be a Father.

And God exercises that power. God is at work in the world. We have to do with God at every turn. God has not abandoned us or the world in which we live. God slumbers not, nor sleeps. One night when Bishop Quayle was so burdened with the problems of the whole world that he could not sleep, he seemed to hear a voice that said to him, "George, why don't you go on to sleep? I'll sit up."

Once again, the power of God is not immediately evident. The riddle of Nickles in Archibald MacLeish's play *J.B.* puts it succinctly: "If God is God [that is, all-powerful], he is not good. If God is good he is not God." Why doesn't God end the misery and the injustice and the pain and the poverty and the strife that warp and twist and dehumanize God's children? Some people have felt that the only way you can defend the morality of God is to say that God really doesn't have the power. Poor, dear God; let's get busy and help God out.

Do you, in spite of all that, believe that God is Almighty? I believe; help my unbelief. One obstacle we can deal with. If God is all-powerful, does that make you powerless? Does this belief reduce you to a puppet, with no power of your own at all? Some have felt so. That would be true if God's power were the power of a tyrant. But God is the Father Almighty. And the power of a Father enhances the power of his children. God does not grow great at our expense; we grow great in God's greatness.

III

"Maker of heaven and earth." What does it mean to say that God is the Creator? It means this universe in which we live is not part of God; it stands over against God; it is other than God. This belief, incidentally, opened the Western world to science. In other cultures, which believed that the universe is somehow part of God, people were forbidden to explore, to dissect, to experiment.

It also means this universe is not an accident; it is not the result of Thomas Hardy's "crass casualty and dicing time"; it is the choice of the Father Almighty. It is here because God intends it to be here and bestows existence and freedom upon it.

You are a part of that creation. So you are not a part of God: you stand over against God; you are other than God. But you are no accident. God made you. God intended you. God risked you. This article of the creed says something tremendous about you—and about every other human being.

We all know this truth is not immediately evident. Other explanations of the universe are quite possible and plausible. It may be just as reasonable to believe in crass casualty and dicing time as in a purposeful Creator.

We have made some very false either-ors with regard to creation. It is not either an observable process or an almighty fiat. An Almighty Father can certainly work in and through a process. No amount of observation of the process can prove or disprove that God is at work in it. You must wager. Was the world made for no reason by nobody? Or was it made for good reasons by God the Father Almighty? The world is full of gods, and new ones are constantly being invented. The Christian faith maintains that the true God, the real God, is God the Father Almighty, Maker of heaven and earth. In that God, in spite of everything, we put our trust.

IV

True faith always brings with it both demand and comfort. The demand is well stated in our Old Testament reading from Malachi: "Have we not all one father? Has not one God created us? Why then are we faithless to one another?" If we say this creed, we obligate ourselves to be faithful to all the other children of our Father and to all the other creatures of our Creator.

The faithlessness at which Malachi aims his attack is faithlessness in marriage, and one could scarcely find a more timely topic. To confess faith in God the Father and then to break faith with that one of God's children to whom we have bound ourselves in covenant—what has come over us? But there is also faithlessness in our business dealings. White-collar crime costs many times over what crimes of violence cost. What constitutes faithfulness when you file form 1040? And there is faithlessness between groups and nations. We all like to find some group or nation not our own whom we can make the scapegoat for the world's ills, as Hitler did to the Jews in Germany. But they are children of the same Father! We can be faithless to the earth and the other creatures by a lifestyle of careless and conspicuous consumption. But air and water and land and animals are creatures of the same Creator! We do well to sweat when we say, "I believe in God the Father Almighty, Maker of heaven and earth."

But there is inexpressible comfort in these words, too. No words of mine can express it as well as the Heidelberg Catechism did over four hundred years ago:

> Q. 26. What do you believe when you say: "I believe in God the Father Almighty, Maker of heaven and earth"?
>
> That the eternal Father of our Lord Jesus Christ, who out of nothing created heaven and earth with all that is in them, who also upholds and governs them by his eternal counsel and providence, is for the sake of Christ his Son my God and my Father. I trust in him so completely that I have no doubt that he will provide me with all things necessary for body and soul. Moreover, whatever evil he sends upon me in this

troubled life he will turn to my good, for he is able to do it, being almighty God, and is determined to do it, being a faithful Father.

Not long ago I was in the presence of a man who believes this. He was staring death in the face, and he said to me, "It's OK. Either way it goes is OK. I'm in God's hands, you know."

We do well to sing, to shout and sing, when we say, "I believe in God the Father Almighty, Maker of heaven and earth."

12

Jesus Christ His Only Son Our Lord

Luke 7:18–23
Hebrews 1:1–4

He was a prisoner. As he walked out into the exercise yard he squinted at the sunlight, for his cell was very dark. Somehow he had escaped the prison barber, and his hair hung long, as he had worn it on the outside: nondescript gray hair against his nondescript gray prison uniform. He had never been fat, but now he was gaunt. He was an organic food man—locusts and wild honey—and he was having real trouble with the potato chips and the greasy hamburgers and the moon pies and all the other junk food they served at the prison mess. Up in the warden's office, the record sheet showed that his name was John. Religious affiliation: Baptist. John the Baptist.

"Hey, Jack!" one of the other cons called to him. "What's your secret? That luscious dame, the warden's stepdaughter, the one that's taking ballet lessons—she's up there watching every time you come out into the exercise yard." John the Baptist kept shuffling and never said a word.

"Hey, Jack!" called another. "Is it true you're a preacher? Are you the one we used to watch on TV, laying down all that line about Jesus?"

Back in the dark of his cell John realized that his arthritis was definitely worse. The corn between his second and third toes was giving him fits. His stomach was churning from his inadequate diet. And his mind was churning from the taunts of his fellow prisoners.

Those had been great days at the big Baptist tabernacle on the banks of the Jordan. They'd brought the crowd in by church buses and school buses from miles around. And the big P.A. system had echoed across the wilderness as he laid a heavy guilt trip on them and then held up to them the one who was to come: Jesus, the Lamb of God; Jesus, the Scourge of God, who would separate the wheat from the chaff and give over the chaff to be burned. And then they turned up the tremolo on the electronic organ, and the finest cantor in Palestine gave out with "How Great Thou Art," and down the aisle they streamed by the thousands!

But now he was in jail and a big rat was scurrying across the floor of his cell. No judgment had fallen on the corrupt political system, where everybody knew that the right to collect taxes was sold to the highest bidder. No judgment had fallen on the archaic, stupid, counterproductive criminal justice system that had him in jail and a klutz like Herod sitting at the warden's desk. And Jesus—Jesus was out there somewhere, wandering around Galilee, telling his parables, healing a few sick, but he wasn't overturning the system, he wasn't shaking the establishment, and he wasn't getting John out of jail or even curing his arthritis or that confounded corn.

The next day, because he knew the prison system and had a little bribe hidden in the camel's-hair coat they let him keep for cold nights, John smuggled out a question for Jesus: "Are you the one who is to come, or should we look for another?"

I

The second article of the Apostles' Creed is the church's answer to John's agonizing question, which is also my agonizing question and perhaps your agonizing question too. We put our trust, with risk and passion, says the creed, "in Jesus Christ his only Son our Lord"—and therefore we do not look for any other.

The first thing that meets us here is a human name:

Jesus. That is the name of a human being, who like all the rest of us lived at a definite place at a definite time, got up in the morning, went to bed at night, ate, drank, and did all the other necessary human things. Jesus is a Jewish name, just another spelling of Joshua. This human being who is mentioned in our creed is a Jew. He is not a Jew by accident, as though he might just as easily have been descended from one of the finest clans of Scotland. He is a Jew by necessity. Only a Jew could have been the Christ.

"Christ" is not a name. Mary never went out in the back yard at Nazareth and called, "Christ, come get your supper!" Christ is a title. It means the Messiah, the anointed one. It is a Jewish title. In ancient Israel, the priests offered the sacrifices, standing before God in behalf of the people and before the people in behalf of God. And priests were anointed. Then there were the prophets, God's mouthpieces. And prophets were anointed. Last, but not least, there were kings and queens, the instruments of God's rule in human history. And kings and queens were anointed.

Now the Christ, the Messiah, is that hoped-for figure who will be Israel's real priest—all that the other priests should have been and never were: Israel's real prophet, Israel's real king. This title brings into our creed God's covenant with Israel, his desire that they be a nation of priests, a royal people, the instrument of God's universal purpose for all nations. And we affirm that in this Jew, Jesus, all this was fulfilled, all the promises of God found their "Yes!" in him.

II

Jesus is the Christ, we declare, and he is God's "only son." Just a minute: God has many children. God is, as we said in the first article, the Father Almighty, the God and Father of us all, whate'er our name or sign. How can Jesus be an only child? In the sense that he is different from the rest of us. That "only" means "the only one of its kind"— God's unique Son.

Hear again the epistle (Heb. 1:1–4): "In many and various ways God spoke of old to our fathers by the prophets; but in these last days he has spoken to us by a Son"—this word that God speaks in the man Jesus is different from all God's other words, because this Word was in the beginning with God, and this Word was God. "Whom he appointed the heir of all things"—the inheritance is his, and it is ours only as he shares it with us. "Through whom also he created the world"—if you draw a line between Creator and creature, there is no question where you and I go: on the creature side; but Jesus is over on the Creator side. "He reflects the glory of God and bears the very stamp of his nature"—you and I are created in God's image, but we are not perfect photocopies; nor do we, to follow the passage on out, uphold the universe by our word of power; we do not make atonement for sins; we do not sit at the right hand of the Majesty on high; we are not superior to the angels.

The uniqueness of Jesus is not, however, a put-down for us. Because he has made common cause with us, because he deigned to become one of us, God's choice of him as his only Son is a choice that also involves us. He is the firstborn of many brothers and sisters. He is the elect Human Being, and in him all humanity is elect.[7]

III

It is this very solidarity with him that leads to the final word: Jesus Christ his only Son "our Lord." He is the head, the chief, the main one, the boss. The buck stops with him; his decisions are final. If we want to be part of his company, we need to get with his program. He stimulates our "loyalty up" by his "loyalty down," remaining faithful, compassionate, and sensitive to the very least one of us, defending us from our enemies and moving us toward the goal.

The Jewish Messiah is now *our* Lord, the Lord of Jews and Gentiles alike, the head of the church in which there have been and always will be both Jewish and Gentile

believers. More than that, he is Lord of the whole world,
even of those who do not believe, Lord of the principalities and powers, Lord of the political system and the criminal justice system. Hear "A Declaration of Faith":

> We declare that Jesus is Lord.
> His resurrection is a decisive victory
>   over the powers that deform and destroy human life.
> His lordship is hidden.
> The world appears to be dominated by people and systems
>   that do not acknowledge his rule.
> But his lordship is real.
> It demands our loyalty and sets us free
>   from the fear of all lesser lords who threaten us.
> We maintain that ultimate sovereignty
>   now belongs to Jesus Christ
>   in every sphere of life.
> Jesus is Lord!
> He has been Lord from the beginning.
> He will be Lord at the end.
> Even now he is Lord.[8]

The church's answer is really something: hammered out
over the years, condensed so every word counts. It needs,
said Calvin, to be sung: yes, and shouted, sounded with
trumpets.

It lays a tremendous obligation on us, of course. "Why
do you call me 'Lord, Lord,' and not do what I tell you?"
(Luke 6:46). Someone has said that modern Christians love
to accept Jesus Christ as Savior (and Lord). The danger is
that at the end, when we come saying, "Lord, Lord," he
will say, "I never knew you; depart from me, you evildo-
ers" (Matt. 7:21, 23). The accent in the creed falls on *Lord*.

IV

But poor old John in his prison did not get the church's
answer, neither the obligation of it nor the glory and the
trumpets. I've often wondered what he made of the answer Jesus sent him. Jesus did not say, "Just hang on for ten
days, or ten years, and that splendid judgment you pre-

dicted will fall. All the Herods will get what's coming to them and all the Johns will be freed and exalted. And everyone will see that I am the Christ, God's only Son, the Lord." He just said, "It's going on, John. A few blind people are seeing what they didn't see before, what they really didn't want to see. A few cripples are walking. Lepers are reentering society. Deaf people are beginning to hear something different from what their local newspaper tells them. Dead people are showing signs of life. And the poor, the poor have good news preached to them. And blessed is the one who chooses to believe rather than to be offended." Why, you know, to some extent, that's going on now, after all these years. There are no trumpets. And what is happening doesn't prove that the second article of the creed is true—not at all—but it holds out the possibility.

I like to think that John saw the possibility and took the risk. I like to think Herod called him and said, "John, tomorrow is my birthday, and I'm feeling generous. If you'll cut your hair and get rid of that old camel's-hair coat and lay off of me about that divorce, and if you'll cool this Jesus-and-judgment business and realize he's just a misguided country preacher, I'll let you out on parole." And John shook his head and said, "No, Herod, Jesus really is the Christ, God's only Son, our Lord." And as he was led back to his cell he saw Salome out of the corner of his eye, practicing the dance of the seven veils.

And then there was Polycarp, the saintly bishop of Smyrna. The Roman soldiers came for him and said, "Old man, you're eighty-six years old. What harm is there in burning incense and saying, 'Caesar is Lord'?" "I can't do it," said the old man, "because Jesus is Lord." And so they lit the kindling around the stake.

And then there was Martin Niemöller, who opposed Hitler and was put in a concentration camp. "Acknowledge the Führer," they told him, "and you'll be released and given command of a U-boat." "Jesus Christ is my Führer," said Niemöller.

What fools they were! And yet—Herod's kingdom is

gone. And the Roman empire is gone. And Hitler's thousand-year Reich is gone. And that strange, quiet kingdom of Jesus, where the blind see and the lame walk and lepers are cleansed and the deaf hear and the dead are raised and good news is preached to the poor—it's still at work here and there, like leaven hidden in three measures of meal, like a seed that grows of itself, we know not how.

So Sunday by Sunday the sermon ends and we stand, some of us welcoming the chance to stretch a bit, others pulling up with some difficulty, children dropping their crayons, some feeling that arthritis more than usual, or that corn between the toes, some maybe even aware that the warden's stepdaughter is looking their way. And we say, as a matter of custom, "I believe . . . in Jesus Christ his only Son our Lord." Do we really? Do you really believe this in the face of the particular Herod who seems to have the power of life and death over you? In the face of the particular Salome who is out to get you? In the face of the bully who picks on you on the playground? In the face of the regulatory agency that is choking your business to death? In the face of a polluted atmosphere that is choking all the rest of us to death? In the face of genocide in Central America and suicide in the U.S.A.? In the face of massed atomic weaponry that can make genocide and suicide global? In the face of the demand that if Jesus is Lord you must do what he says?

Yes, we do believe it. There is that music in the background behind and underneath all the noise of our lives. Any time we quiet down we can hear it:

> King of Kings and Lord of Lords,
> and he shall reign for ever and ever.

Lord, we believe; help our unbelief.

13

Conceived by
the Holy Ghost

Isaiah 11:1–9
Luke 1:26–35

At her trial before the King of Hearts, Alice in Wonderland was handed a paper to read. "Where shall I begin, your majesty?" she asked. "Begin at the beginning and read through to the end," he replied gravely. That's not always good advice. Some things are understood better if we begin at the end and work back to the beginning. That strikes me as the best approach to our subject now.

I

So we begin with the common life of the church—the life of the church that began on the Day of Pentecost. Here were people who were deeply stirred; the depths of their lives had been broken up and they were feeling and experiencing new and unexpected things. Here were people who were strongly drawn to each other in a profound unity that embraced and overcame all their diversity; the barriers between them were down. Here were people mightily empowered for their mission to the world. And those first Christians understood very well that they had been swept by the winds of the Holy Spirit, set on fire by the flames of the Holy Spirit. The Agent of God's presence and power that had visited God's ancient people now and then had come to rest and abide with them.

They had another conviction. It was Jesus Christ, God's

only Son our Lord, who had bestowed on them this marvelous gift. Peter put it this way in his sermon on Pentecost: "This Jesus God raised up, and of that we all are witnesses. Being therefore exalted at the right hand of God, and having received from the Father the promise of the Holy Spirit, he has poured out this which you see and hear" (Acts 2:32–33). So they had no hesitation in calling the Holy Spirit the Spirit of Jesus, the Spirit of Christ.

Now we begin to move back toward the beginning. If Jesus is the bestower of the Spirit, he must also have been the bearer of the Spirit.[9] If he possesses the Spirit and gives it to the church, he must himself have been possessed by the Spirit. He must have been stirred in his depths, drawn out in love, empowered mightily by the Spirit. Had not Isaiah prophesied of the Messiah, the Christ: "The Spirit of the LORD shall rest upon him, the spirit of wisdom and understanding, the spirit of counsel and might, the spirit of knowledge and the fear of the LORD" (Isa. 11:2)?

Now then, when did the Spirit of the Lord begin to rest upon Jesus? At what point in his life did this power begin to work in him? When was his Pentecost? The most obvious suggestion is the resurrection. When he was raised from the dead, no longer in the flesh, Jesus began an existence controlled and saturated with the Holy Spirit. The words of Peter quoted earlier seem to point to this understanding, and so do other New Testament passages, such as Paul's words that Jesus was "descended from David according to the flesh and designated Son of God in power according to the Spirit of holiness by his resurrection from the dead" (Rom. 1:3–4).

But don't we have to go back further? Did not Jesus perform his earthly ministry in the power of the Holy Spirit? Of course he did. It was by the Spirit of God that he cast out the unclean spirits. The words that he spoke were Spirit and life. In his movements about Galilee he was led and driven by the Spirit.

So we move back to the baptism. At the very beginning of his ministry, Jesus comes up from the water and the heavens open and the Holy Spirit descends on him in form like a dove. That must be when it happened.

But what about the first thirty years of his life: his babyhood, his boyhood, his adolescence, the long quiet years at Nazareth when he lived as a common worker, earning bread by the sweat of his brow amid the sawdust and shavings of a carpenter shop? That is where he became the person he was at his baptism, a fit vessel for the Spirit's power. Did he do all that on his own?

You see, the problem with placing Jesus' personal Pentecost at his resurrection or at his baptism is that he thereby becomes God's *adopted* Son. That means there is a first stage, either thirty years or thirty-three years of human life, in which Jesus makes it on his own. He does it so well that God says, "Look, what a magnificent human being! I'll adopt him as my Son and bestow my Spirit upon him."

No, we must move on back to that story where the angel Gabriel is sent to Mary to tell her, "The Holy Spirit will come upon you, and the power of the Most High will overshadow you; therefore the child to be born will be called holy, the Son of God" (Luke 1:35). And out of that story we must declare in our creed, "He was conceived by the Holy Ghost."

Jesus can bestow the Holy Spirit on us because he was the bearer of the Spirit from birth—and even from before birth, from conception. There is no portion of Jesus' life where the initiative is not God's. He is no two-stage rocket—first human, then divine—but one glorious explosion, which is what a conception is. And there is that moment, so mysterious in your life and mine, even more mysterious in his, when out of the incalculable, indefinite possibilities of what a given life might be, one definite potential is chosen and the individual's uniqueness is set, forever different now from anyone else at all. There in that moment the Holy Spirit, God's initiative, was shaping, forming, attending.

So Jesus is not the upthrust of humanity toward God, the

best we could produce. He is the downthrust of God into our common humanity. Not even Jesus was saved by works, by human initiative and effort. He is the supreme example of grace—God's loving us, God's stooping to our needs. His human life from its very inception is at the same time God's life among us. He was conceived by the Holy Ghost.

II

How does it make you feel to stand up in church and, along with everybody else, to say, "I believe he was conceived by the Holy Ghost"? I have very mixed feelings. On one side I'm thrilled and excited: all the trumpets are sounding. At least once there was on this planet a human life that was all it ought to be, from its very beginning to its very end, a life filled with the Spirit from the moment of conception. But on the other side I am driven to despair because my life falls so far short of that one. The humanity of Jesus inspires me, but it also judges my humanity. I look back on all the times I have tried to make a new start. I have sat down and confessed my laziness, my prayerlessness, my lack of discipline, my lovelessness, my selfishness. I am depressed at my inability to become what I know I ought to be and what, at least in part, I desperately want to be. So I have taken out my little notebook and written up a new plan, a new schedule, a new spiritual discipline. And I've known, even as I wrote, that I'd fall by the wayside, that I wouldn't be able to carry it out for long. And there's Jesus, just living a truly spiritual life from the moment of his conception. "Woe is me . . . for I am a man of unclean lips, and I dwell in the midst of a people of unclean lips; for my eyes have seen the King!" (Isa. 6:5).

More and more, as my life races by at an ever accelerating pace, I find myself identifying with Nicodemus: that old theologian, that old churchman, who skipped session meeting one night and went to see Jesus, drawn by the life of the Spirit that he saw in him, and despairing of his own life. And he asked Jesus, "How can a man be born when he is old? Can he enter a second time into his mother's womb and be born?" (John 3:4).

Do you identify there, too? Is our spiritual life a long series of defeats and are you conscious of growing older all the time? In the Pennsylvania Dutch country they sell tourists little wall plaques that say, "We grow too soon old und too late schmart." I want to hang on my wall one that says, "We grow too soon old and too late devout, too late filled with the Holy Spirit."

III

God has the wildest sense of humor. Do you remember what Jesus replied to Nicodemus? He told him one can be born of water and the Spirit. The water of baptism—so public, so visible, so ordinary in its way—is the outward sign of a believer's reconception and rebirth by the Holy Spirit. In addition to our natural conception by our father and mother, which sets our hereditary patterns and makes us uniquely who we are, there is also a conception by the Holy Spirit in our baptism. And alongside our natural lives, there develops within each one of us a silent, secret life of the Spirit, often not visible to others or even to ourselves— what Henry Scougal called "The Life of God in the Soul of Man." We do not earn this any more than Jesus did. I suspect that our schedules, disciplines, notebooks, our secret pride and open despair, have very little to do with this hidden life within us.

One of the great mistakes, as I see it, in the charismatic movement of our day is that so many ignore this long, silent growth of the spiritual life, so many discount their Nazareth years. When some exciting spiritual experience comes, they declare that at last they have received the Spirit, been baptized by the Spirit; they have never really experienced the Spirit before. This is a destructive and divisive misunderstanding.

Every believer, and every child of believers, has within her, within him, a life conceived by the Holy Ghost. We are all in process of becoming children of God, who are born "not of blood nor of the will of the flesh nor of the will of man, but of God" (John 1:12–13).

We are all conscious of that life in ourselves and in others which is not spiritual at all, which is of the will of the flesh. I remember a woman in my first parish who went to a summer conference. She reported to me, "They told us there to live for the honor of Jesus, and I came home determined to be just as honor-y as I can!" She succeeded. Any pastor is aware of and depressed by the orneriness of some of his or her members. But then a crisis comes, and that member's soul is laid bare. And there it is: a courage, a tenderness, a peace, a resignation to the will of God, an ability to drink the cup, that one would never have imagined—the life of God in the human soul. And the sensitive pastor quietly removes his or her shoes, standing on holy ground.

This insight that there is in us, too, a life conceived by the Holy Spirit has greatly aided my understanding of communion. As we gather at the table we see all too clearly each other's fleshly lives, what was conceived by our fathers and mothers, what irritates us in others and shames us in ourselves. And we wonder, How can we eat and drink together? How can Christ invite us here?

The answer is that Christ sees that hidden life in us that is generated by his Holy Spirit. The Spirit that conceived him has reconceived us. Each person at the table is a battleground of the flesh versus the Spirit and the Spirit versus the flesh. Our Captain offers us battle rations. These tiny portions of bread and wine do little for our bodies. They are the food of our hidden lives, of that in us which has been conceived by the Holy Spirit.

14

Born of the Virgin Mary

Matthew 1:18–25

Guerrilla warfare is nothing new. It broke out often between the tribes and subgroups of ancient Israel. One time the Gileadites held the fords of the Jordan against the Ephraimites. The Ephraimites had to cross the Jordan to get home, so they'd approach the Gileadite sentries and say, "I'm no Ephraimite." "All right," the Gileadites would reply, "say Shibboleth." And the Ephraimites, with their incurable southern accents, would say, "Sibboleth." So the record says that 42,000 Ephraimites were slain at the fords of the Jordan because they could not frame their mouths to pronounce the word right.

In the guerrilla warfare that has divided American Protestants since around 1890 and continues today, the virgin birth has been the shibboleth. Say "virgin birth," and you're OK. Refuse to say it, and you're done for. We may not slay you at the fords of the Jordan, but we will call you a modernist, a liberal, an unbeliever; we will be sure you're no Christian; we will preach sermons against you in which we will warn people not to listen to you and assure them you are bound straight for hell.

Now that long and continuing history has to be in my mind as I approach, with some fear and trembling, this phrase in our series on the Apostles' Creed, "Born of the Virgin Mary."

I

The first thing I want to say is that it's the wrong shibboleth. I can agree with the intent of the fundamentalists and the evangelicals. They are concerned for the deity of Christ. Jesus Christ is more than a great human teacher, more than a splendid human example, more than a noble human martyr. His life among us was at the same time God's life among us. However that truth may offend people, we must say it if we want to talk about Christianity. But "born of the Virgin Mary" is the wrong shibboleth for that purpose.

The Apostles' Creed contains much stronger and clearer affirmations of the deity of Christ than the words "born of the Virgin Mary." The deity of Christ is more strongly affirmed in the words "conceived by the Holy Ghost." It is even more strongly affirmed in "sitteth on the right hand of God." And the strongest, most basic affirmation is the one that opens the second article: "Jesus Christ, his only Son, our Lord." It is simply true that the words "born of the Virgin Mary" could be entirely omitted from the creed, and the deity of Christ would still be affirmed with great strength.

To make the virgin birth the shibboleth of Christ's deity is not only to misunderstand the creed but to misunderstand scripture as well. The stories of the virgin birth in Matthew and Luke are clearly part of scripture, a beautiful and moving part. But scripture does not depend on those stories to establish the deity of Christ. The great affirmations of the deity of Christ are found in the letters of Paul and in the Gospel of John and in the epistle to the Hebrews—and in none of those do you find the story of the virgin birth. It is simply true that the stories of the virgin birth could be entirely omitted from scripture and the deity of Christ would still be affirmed with great strength.

To quiz someone about his or her belief in the virgin birth—to hold that up as the shibboleth—may reveal something about his or her attitude toward biological miracles or toward biblical criticism, but it will not reveal very much regarding his or her attitude toward the deity of Christ. It is the wrong shibboleth.

History is a strange mixture of tragedy and comedy, and church history is the most tragic and the most comic. The selection of the virgin birth around 1890 as the shibboleth has in some ways been tragic. In my hometown I watched an evangelist fill his tent night after night by destroying the reputation and effectiveness of the YMCA secretary in that town, one of the most devout and creative Christians I have ever known—because the YMCA secretary would not say the shibboleth. Those tragic stories could be multiplied a hundred times, a thousand times.

The comedy is that those who place themselves in the role of defenders of the faith, holding the fords of the Jordan against the unbelieving Ephraimites, betray to all who have eyes to see it an amazing ignorance of what the virgin birth has meant down through the history of the church.

II

That leads to the second thing I want to say. Making a shibboleth of the virgin birth has robbed us of the great positive values, the great theological treasures, that are there for us in the words "born of the Virgin Mary."

When the Apostles' Creed was originally formed, the emphasis was on the word "born." Jesus, who is the Christ, who is God's only son, who is our Lord, who was conceived by the Holy Ghost, was born! He came into the world through the process of human birth. The great issue at that time was whether the Son of God could really be involved in genuine, earthy, flesh-and-blood existence. There were many who said no: God is spirit and can have no connection with flesh and blood. Some even said the true God didn't create this material world. It was a false God who did that. Our pure souls are trapped in our foul bodies. The Son of God came down to free us from all this stuff. So of course he wasn't born. He wasn't involved in the painful, messy process of human birth. He fell to earth like a ray of sunlight. He only seemed to have a body. He only seemed to suffer. He only seemed to die. It is against this hyperspirituality that the creed says, firmly and simply, "He was born of the Virgin Mary." This phrase is the great defense of the earthiness, the fleshliness, the genuine humanity of Jesus. It was so understood by the Reformers and by most major theologians down to the nineteenth century.

This phrase not only emphasizes the reality of Jesus' humanity, it emphasizes his humiliation. In Philippians 2, Paul quotes an early Christian hymn. That hymn clearly demonstrates that the shape of the Christian story is a parabola, with a descent and an ascent, humiliation and exaltation. Jesus, it says, was in the form of God. But he did not grasp at his equality with God. He emptied himself and took the form of a servant. He was born in the likeness of humanity. So "he humbled himself and became obedient unto death, even death on a cross. Therefore God has highly exalted him and bestowed on him the name which is above every name, that at the name of Jesus every knee should bow . . . and every tongue confess that Jesus Christ is Lord, to the glory of God the Father" (Phil. 2:5–11). Now the virgin birth is not part of the exaltation, it is part of the humiliation.

The Westminster divines understood this very well. Larger Catechism, Question 47: "How did Christ humble himself in his conception and birth?" Answer: "Christ humbled himself in his conception and birth, in that, being from all eternity the Son of God in the bosom of the Father, he was pleased in the fullness of time to become the Son of man, made of a woman of low estate, and to be born to her, with divers circumstances of more than ordinary abasement." Those "divers circumstances" included being born in a stable of a mother who became pregnant before she was married and incurred the normal suspicions, including the suspicion of her own husband-to-be. It was humbling enough for the Son of God to be born as a human being, but he went further and humbled himself to be born in circumstances like that. And all for you and me.

The virgin birth unfolds the humanity of Jesus and his gracious humiliation for our sakes, but the most precious treasure of all is the necessity of human cooperation in God's work.

Presumably God could have sent the Messiah down from heaven full grown, clothed in armor, at the head of a troop of angels, with no help from any human being whatsoever. But God doesn't work that way.

God chooses to be dependent on our human responses to the divine initiative. The initiative is God's. We need to be clear about that. We don't generate God's purposes, plan how God is to carry them out, and then issue God orders.

> God moves in a mysterious way
> God's wonders to perform.[10]

But in God's movements God asks for and awaits and depends on our human response to the divine initiative.

What the virgin birth teaches us is that Jesus could not have been born, God's great central purpose in history could not have been achieved, if there had not been a simple peasant girl who was willing to respond to God's initiative, to face all the pain, all the risk, all the unknown, all the suspicion, all the shame, and say, "Behold . . . the handmaid of the Lord. Let it be to me according to your word" (Luke 1:38).

III

At the very beginning of this series we said that "I believe" means "I put my trust, I wager my life, with risk and passion." What is it that I put my trust in when I say Jesus was "born of the Virgin Mary"? Do I wager my life on the nonpaternity of Joseph? That is part of the story, but my salvation does not rest on that. It rests rather on the human cooperation of Mary with God's initiative and plan. As bad as the human race is, there are some human beings who cooperate with the purposes of God, and chief among them is Mary. Her human name is here in the creed to remind me that my trust is not only in God but also in God's human cooperators. When I say "born of the Virgin Mary," I am through with a cozy little private religion—"Just you and me, God, just you and me." I acknowledge my dependence on my brothers and sisters in the faith, and especially on this sister.

I find that exciting. I find it liberating. I find it mind-blowing. "Born of the Virgin Mary"—that's far too precious to use as a weapon to guard the fords of the Jordan. It's not a weapon. It's a rose.

> Isaiah 'twas foretold it,
> The rose I have in mind,
> With Mary we behold it,
> The Virgin Mother kind.
> To show God's love aright
> She bore to us a Saviour,
> When half spent was the night.[11]

15

Suffered Under Pontius Pilate

Matthew 27:11–26

It is a moment in Dorothy Sayers's radio drama, *The Man Born to Be King.* The crucifixion is in progress. Back in the governor's palace, Pilate is asking his wife to tell him more about her bad dream of the night before. Her dream, she says, was filled with a phrase, spoken by a thousand voices in a hundred different languages over and over again: "Suffered under Pontius Pilate, suffered under Pontius Pilate, suffered under Pontius Pilate."

That bad dream has become literal fact. Almost two thousand years later the name of Pontius Pilate is still remembered. And daily in Pilate's own Latin, and in English, German, French, Spanish, Chinese, Japanese, Hindi, Swahili—in the whole Babel of human languages—that phrase is repeated: "Suffered under Pontius Pilate, suffered under Pontius Pilate, suffered under Pontius Pilate."

I

Strange: he was not famous in his own day but one of a hundred petty provincial governors in the Roman bureaucracy. He was not a brave man, not a strong man, but actually a very weak man. He knew Jesus was innocent. He said so, publicly, many times during the trial. Yet in the end he condemned him and permitted him to suffer the irreversible penalty of capital punishment.

John Calvin said an interesting thing about us human beings and our sense of justice. Even after our nature has been corrupted by the fall and by original sin, he said, we still possess a very accurate sense of justice—until our own interests are involved. In general, in detachment, in matters that do not involve our own honor or our own money, jobs, affections, or ambitions, we can see instantly what justice demands. But when our own interests enter the situation, our judgment is warped, twisted, and distorted and we can sanction the grossest injustice.

So it was with Pilate. In the finest tradition of Roman law he saw instantly where justice lay in the case of Jesus. The man was clearly innocent. But then the high priests brought Pilate's own interest in: "If you release this man you are not Caesar's friend." If he did justice, he could be accused of coddling criminals, of being weak on law and order, of sympathizing with subversives, of disloyalty to Caesar, of imperiling national security. He could lose his job and his civil service rating. He could end his career in disgrace. So he called for water and washed his hands. Scrub them, Pilate! Pour on the soap and the detergent. Shakespeare's Macbeth will tell you the results:

> Will all great Neptune's ocean wash this blood
> Clean from my hand? No, this my hand will rather
> The multitudinous seas incarnadine,
> Making the green one red.[12]

So Pilate washed. And so he gave in and ordered injustice done. He had no idea he was stumbling into the Apostles' Creed.

II

We meet him all the time. I sat in his courtroom in Alabama back in the fifties. Willie, a young black man, one of my students, was accused of whistling and making gestures at a white girl. Willie testified he never saw the white girl; he was calling to his friend Eddie. This Pilate was a big, likable bear of a man who knew instantly where justice lay. There was really no law against whistling, and Willie had indeed been looking in Eddie's direction. But the girl's relatives were all there, red-necked and hot-eyed. The real power in the town was held by the White Citizens Council and the Ku Klux Klan. His job was at stake. So injustice was done to an innocent party.

We meet him all the time. He sits year after year in the U.S. Senate. He knows that most homicides in this country result not from the attacks of strangers but from quarrels between members of the same family and between friends. He knows that the availability of handguns often makes the difference between a quarrel and a homicide. He knows that almost every law enforcement official in the land favors a tighter control on handguns. He knows that an overwhelming majority of citizens favor gun control. But he also knows that one of the most powerful lobbies in the land dumped a thousand letters on his desk in the preceding week. He knows they could mark him for defeat in his reelection and that the vote goes their way almost every time. So he gets up nervously and walks out to the washroom and washes his hands. Then he comes back and votes to weaken an already weak gun control law.

We meet her all the time. She sits on the board of a powerful corporation. She has just been informed that the plant on which the company has staked its future and into which it has already poured vast funds presents a remote but real peril of terrifying proportions. She grasps, as well as any human mind can grasp such things, the enormity of that remote danger to all our grandchildren, including her own. What justice demands is clear to her, but vast interests—her interests—are involved. She walks out to the marble executive washroom and washes her hands. Then she comes back and votes to suppress the information about the danger.

We meet him all the time. I meet Pontius Pilate in my mirror. Oh, yes, there's the bold preacher who points out our national and corporate and individual sins like one of the old prophets—until my own interest is involved. And at that point justice becomes blurred and indistinct, and I am tempted to be very accommodating.

The truth is, in all places and times in human history, the kingdoms of this world are ruled by Pontius Pilate—occasionally by titans and tyrants, the Caesars and Napoleons and Hitlers, but usually by decent, average people who can see and do justice well enough—until their own interest is involved.

III

Why should the name of Pilate be in our creed? To pass from "Jesus Christ his only Son our Lord; who was conceived by the Holy Ghost, born of the Virgin Mary"—to pass from that to "suffered under Pontius Pilate" is like being in an elegant church when an old cur dog wanders down the aisle. What is there in this flat historical statement that we need to believe, to wager our lives on with risk and passion?

Precisely because it is a flat historical statement, that phrase anchors our Christian faith in human history. It rules out conclusively all attempts to make Christianity a pie-in-the-sky religion, a trip to some never-never land, a fairy tale that happened once upon a time. When we say this name of Pilate we state our faith that Christianity is *historical,* its hinge and pivot is an event of history that occurred at a definite time and place: about A.D. 30, when Pilate was governor; in Judea, which is the place he governed. That year, A.D. 30, is on exactly the same calendar that now contains the month and day and year of today's newspaper. And that Judea is on exactly the same map that marks your hometown. This we believe, with risk and passion.

And by believing it, we believe something deeper. We believe that when God's only Son chose to come into the world, it was the kind of world we still live in. It was a world ruled and controlled by people who knew justice and did injustice, just as the rulers of the world still do a great deal of the time, even today. Jesus knew a world with

Pilate in control—the world you and I live in now. He put up with it, he endured it, he remained true to God in it. It did him in, but just when it thought it had him, he conquered it.

"In the world you have tribulation," he told his disciples, and he tells you and me; "but be of good cheer, I have overcome the world" (John 16:33).

Lord, we believe; help our unbelief.

16

Crucified, Dead, and Buried

Mark 15:20–47

Crucified, dead, and buried. At this point the Apostles' Creed becomes gloomy indeed. The words would stick in our throats if we did not slide them out by long familiarity. We don't want to hear that Jesus, the Christ, God's only Son, our Lord, not only suffered the trauma and indignity of human birth, not only suffered the oppression and injustice of human government, personified by Pontius Pilate, but suffered the unspeakable torture of crucifixion, suffered death, and suffered the final indignity of burial in the ground.

We don't like to hear that because it seems unfair, absurd, and demeaning for such things to happen to the Son of God. We can understand those Christians of the second century who wanted to rewrite the whole story and say that God's spiritual and immaterial Son came to earth like a ray of sunshine. He only appeared to have a physical body; he was too spiritual for that. He only appeared to be hungry and tired and sad and angry, for a divine being can only know joy and bliss. So at the end he could not have hung there on the cross. No, he escaped back into heaven and the soldiers took poor old Simon of Cyrene, a black man who was passing by, and crucified him.

The creed won't let us engage in such foolishness. No, Jesus Christ, God's only Son, our Lord, was *crucified*—we acknowledge the barbarous manner of his death; he was *dead*—brute fact of his death; he was *buried*—the final consequence and consummation of his death. Some have asked why the creed is so repetitious here. If he was crucified, he was obviously dead; and if he was dead, he was surely buried. But the creed says it three times—dead, dead, dead—like the tolling of a death bell.

"Never send to know for whom the bell tolls; it tolls for thee."[13] And that's the other reason we do not like to hear these gloomy words. Our own crucifixion, our own death, our own burial are involved. Jesus endured these terrible things as a part of his complete entry into the human condition—your condition and mine.

We do not want to hear these words, but we must hear all three, one at a time, if we are to be true to the creed.

I

Crucified. Jesus was not the only one ever crucified. Two others were crucified that same day. Hundreds, perhaps thousands of Jews were crucified by the Romans. There was not a year of Jesus' life on earth in which some of his fellow Jews were not executed in this cruel and barbarous way by the Roman overlords.

Crucifixion is a form of capital punishment in which the state asserts its right to take life, although no individual has that right. It is irremediable punishment. If later on it turns out that the accused was innocent, it's just tough. Without going into the gory details, which are well enough known, we can say that crucifixion is capital punishment by torture. It is the awful surfeit of pain and agony that brings death.

Crucifixion is not widely practiced today, but capital punishment and torture are. There are many people in our world for whom execution and torture are daily possibilities of their lives. Have you ever thought of the possibility that you might be executed or tortured? The odds may be very, very small, being who you are and where you are on the economic and power scales. But if you are poor, unlettered, and black, the odds will be more considerable. And if you live in Cambodia or Central America, if you are black or "colored" and want freedom in South Africa, if you live under military dictatorship in South America or North Korea or Central Africa—the possibility of execution and torture is frightening indeed.

Now when we say the creed we declare that Jesus was crucified. That possibility, so remote for some, less remote for others, became an actuality for him. There is no one endangered by the cruelest regime, no one whether innocent or guilty, who can say of Jesus, "He does not know the trouble I've seen; I have no part in him and he has no part in me." He, the Son of God, was crucified.

II

Dead. Here we move from possibility to certainty. Have you thought about the certainty of your own death? Most of us haven't. During World War II a Marine division was being briefed regarding a landing on one of the South Pacific islands. "Our artillery," they were told, "has been unable to dislodge the Japanese. When the first wave hits the beach probably only five out of a hundred will survive." "Gee," said a Marine private, 'I'm gonna miss all those other guys." We are all like that: undaunted in our confidence that we will survive.

Our culture, like no other culture in history perhaps, helps us maintain our unreality about death. Dr. Elisabeth Kubler-Ross got started in her well-known work in the area of death and dying when a seminary student asked her to help him with a project. She asked the great hospital adjacent to the University of Chicago to let her and the student talk to three or four dying patients. The request threw the hospital into utter confusion. Finally they replied, "We have no dying patients." Hundreds of hospital beds and no dying patients? The denial of death is stoutly maintained by those who deal with it daily.

Yet the most certain of all certainties is our death. And Jesus experienced that certainty. He really died. His life came to a crunching end—finis, kaput, all over, three strikes and you're out. Dead, dead, dead.

When death comes to you in a hospice, or suddenly out of the blue, or when you are yoked to a dozen machines, you cannot say that Jesus does not know what you are experiencing, that he has no part in you or you in him. He, our Lord, was dead.

III

Buried. The final insult. The most beautiful, marvelous, and intricate thing that God ever made, the human body—when the life goes out of it—becomes a problem, a nuisance, a threat, an unbearable burden to those left alive. So it must be put out of sight, put in the ground, buried. There is the slow procession to the cemetery, the customary words are said, the crowd lingers to greet one another, and then everyone leaves but one. Has it ever occurred to you that one day you will be that one? That day came for Jesus. He was buried.

Now then, why should we stand up in church Sunday after Sunday and affirm that we believe such bad news— bad news about the Son of God, bad news about the human condition, bad news about ourselves?

For one thing, only if we are honest about the bad news can we begin to hear the good news. The resurrection has no meaning to those who are dishonest about the reality of human suffering and death. If Jesus was not really human, if he did not really suffer, if he did not really die, what does Easter amount to? Very little. If he escaped and poor old Simon of Cyrene died, what does the empty tomb amount to? Nothing at all. It is pointless.

These three words forever fence out the forms of Christianity that ignore tragedy: Yoga Christianity—do these meditations and exercises and you will escape the storm of life; success Christianity—tithe and do right and you will always be prosperous, happy, and successful; sweetness-and-light Christianity—it's all in your mind, so think positive thoughts and nothing bad will happen to you. No, no, no. In true Christianity, the tragedy comes first, then the comedy; the bad news, then the good news.

The longer I live the more clearly I see that it is our denial of the negatives, of the dark side of life, that keeps us from hearing the gospel. Real Christianity has the courage to take the world as it is, to see that we are all of us the poor naked creatures of *King Lear,* caught in the pitiless storm, with only "looped and windowed raggedness" to protect us. Christ comes out into the storm as naked and helpless as the rest of us, enduring it until it destroys him. And *then,* he rose again from the dead and sitteth on the right hand of God the Father Almighty. *Then* nothing can separate us from the love of God, neither death nor life nor angels nor principalities nor powers, nor the pelting of the pitiless storm, nor anything. *Then* we shall be like him, for we shall see him as he is; having been conformed to his suffering, we shall be conformed to his glory.

There is a deeper reason still why we affirm this bad news, Sunday after Sunday. Interestingly, the Apostles' Creed scarcely hints at it. We have to turn to that other ancient creed, the Nicene Creed, to get it clear: "Who for us . . . and for our salvation, came down from heaven . . . and was crucified also for us under Pontius Pilate."

The "for us" is the point. That opens up the whole business of the atonement, the details of which we cannot enter into here. Let us hold to the simple words of a hymn written for children:

> There is a green hill far away,
>   Outside a city wall,
> Where the dear Lord was crucified,
>   Who died to save us all.

> We may not know, we cannot tell,
>   What pains He had to bear;
> But we believe it was for us
>   He hung and suffered there.[14]

That's what makes the bad news the very best news of all.
  Lord, we believe; help our unbelief.

17

He Descended Into Hell

Hebrews 4:14—5:10

We have already said that the second article of the Apostles' Creed—the part about Jesus Christ—is shaped like a parabola. It descends from glory into deeper and deeper humiliation, and then it turns and ascends once again into greater and greater glory.

When we dealt with "crucified, dead, and buried," it must have seemed that we had hit bottom. Humiliation was complete. There's no way from there but up. And then the creed hands us this: "He descended into hell."

I face a great temptation not to deal with that terrible phrase. For one thing, it crept into the creed very late, not before the fifth century. For four centuries the church said this creed in various forms, but without ever saying, "He descended into hell." That other ancient creed, the great Nicene Creed, is patterned on the Apostles' Creed, but there is nothing in the Nicene Creed to correspond to those dread words, "He descended into hell." There is still no solid agreement among Christians as to what these words meant in the first place. Did they refer to a trip Jesus took in the spirit during the three days his body lay in the tomb? Or did they refer, as the Larger Catechism (Q. 50) puts it, to his "continuing in the state of the dead, and under the power of death till the third day"? Some Christians have found in these words a basis for believing in purgatory and limbo and all kinds of things other Christians don't believe in. We can certainly understand the footnote in many hymnbooks: "Some churches omit this."

I

Let's face it. There are tremendous difficulties here for modern people. It is here that we meet head on "the three-story universe": Heaven—up there; earth—here; and hell—down there. We simply cannot take that literally. We live on a ball that rotates on its axis and revolves around the sun, traveling with it through the vast reaches of space. "Up" will be a different direction an hour from now, for the earth will have rotated. Within twenty-four hours it will have been all different directions. And "down" is even more mysterious. We know more about stars trillions of miles away than about the core of our own planet, a very few miles under our feet. Because, of course, we can see the stars, and we have not yet penetrated much below the crust of earth. We do know it's hot down there, though we can only speculate on the amount of heat and the source of the heat. We shall continue to pursue the problem, but we will be looking for a source of geothermal energy, not for the hollow halls of hell, peopled by Satan and his minions and countless numbers of the earth's dead.

What do we do when we can no longer accept an ancient statement, a statement rich in meaning to long generations before us, as an accurate description of reality out there? We can junk the statement, as many have done. Many in our generation have dismissed the church as a stronghold of unscientific superstition. Others come and cannot say the creed. "I would lose my integrity," one told me, "if I stood up and joined in that medieval nonsense." Or we can ask this ancient statement a different question. Granted it is not a reliable report of the reality out there, what does it say to the reality in here, to me as a person, to my existence as a woman or a man?

II

If we take this last course, we are seized and shaken. "He descended into hell" means Jesus has entered into the final depths and dregs of my most negative experience. It means Jesus, too, knows about the absence of God.

For in scripture, hell—or Sheol, as the Old Testament calls it—is the final and irremediable absence of God. It is to be cut off from the hand of God and remembered by God no more (Ps. 88:5). God works no wonders there, and those in hell do not rise up to praise God (Ps. 88:10). God's steadfast love is not declared there, and God's faithfulness is unknown (Ps. 88:11). Hell is where not even God can help me anymore.

We do not, of course, have to wait until after death to experience the absence of God. It's a part of the life we know now. We tend to read our Bibles so optimistically we fail to see that scripture is shot through with the absence of God. "And the word of the LORD was rare in those days," we read; "there was no frequent vision" (1 Sam. 3:1). Amos speaks of a famine of the word of the Lord: "They shall wander from sea to sea, and from north to east; they shall run to and fro, to seek the word of the LORD, but they shall not find it" (Amos 8:12). "Oh, that I knew where I might find him!" cries Job (23:3). And the psalmist says, "My tears have been my food day and night, while [they] say to me continually, 'Where is your God?'" (Ps. 42:3). And the prophet cries, "Truly, thou art a God who hidest thyself!" (Isa. 45:15).

The absence of God is the great agony of the people of God. Those who are not God's people are glad enough to have God out of the way. But the people of God, who know that life is drawn from God and without God there is no life—they are in agony over the absence of God. They know that the presence of God is a gift, not a right we can demand. God comes like rain at the end of a long drought, like a child to a woman who has been barren for years, like a feast at the end of a famine. The people of God are sustained, not so much by God's actual presence as by the hope of it: for God comes, to judge the world with righteousness and the peoples with truth (Ps. 96:13).

I meet people who say they live daily and hourly in God's presence. I have no criticism. It must be wonderful. But I must testify that I live a great part of the time in God's absence. And I suspect that many of you, if you were honest, would testify the same.

People live in hell right now. I think of the number of people I know who suffer some kind of addiction. Alcohol, or some other drug, has moved into the very center of their lives, and rules. God is absent, for God's proper place has been usurped by the addiction. And they live daily and hourly in hell. I think of the masses of oppressed people, on both sides of all the world's curtains: how often they describe their existence—stripped of dignity, denied freedom, living in constant fear—as "hell." I think of the number of people I know who are trapped in malignant personal relationships, caught in endless dishonest games, grappling in bonds of mutual loathing. They know the truth that is in Sartre's play *No Exit:* hell is other people. I think of depressed people, caught in a downward spiral of self-hatred, down, down, down, until there seems no way of reaching God and no way God can reach them.

It is ironic, isn't it, that in an age where the old idea of hell has become untenable, these existential hells are more widely prevalent than ever before? The chorus rises from a thousand throats all about us: "My God, my God, why hast thou forsaken me?"

III

Where have you heard that before? On the lips of the Son of God (Matt. 27:46; Mark 15:34).

Jesus was one who lived in the constant presence of God. "My food," he said, "is to do the will of [the one] who sent me" (John 4:34). "I am in the Father and the Father in me" (John 14:10). "I am not alone, for the Father is with me" (John 16:32). If he had died in the complete comfort of that presence, and risen again to resume that sweet fellowship, could he have helped those of us who know the absence of God? Oh, yes, he would have taken our flesh, endured the trauma of human birth, suffered the political oppression of Pilate, felt the pain of physical torture, the disgrace of capital punishment, the finality of death, the shame of burial. But would he have known the sharpest thing of all—the absence of God, when the heavens above are brass, when God hears nothing, speaks nothing, is nowhere around?

"He descended into hell." Jesus does know the absence of God before death and the absence of God after death in the grave. How one who was God's Son, very God of very God, could know the absence of God is a mystery I cannot fathom. But his humanity was so real, he was so much one of us, that he knew it, knew it in the very depths of his being.

Now we are ready for that utterly fantastic passage from Hebrews. "Although he was a Son, he learned obedience through what he suffered"—learned it just as you and I learn it. "He offered up prayers and supplications, with loud cries and tears"—he cried in a loud voice, *"Eloi, eloi, lama sabachthani?"* ("My God, my God, why hast thou forsaken me?"). "He was heard for his godly fear"—God heard him even though he didn't know God heard him. "We have not a high priest who is unable to sympathize with our weaknesses, but one who in every respect has been tempted as we are"—even to the absence of God, the living hell—"yet without sin."

IV

In his great little book *Guilt and Redemption,* Lewis Sherrill has a chapter entitled "The Descent Into Hell." It is a description of psychotherapy, or of what psychotherapy ought to be. The therapist, says Sherrill, descends with you into your private hell, goes with you as, a step at a time, you dig into what you have been unable to deal with and unwilling to face. The therapist never condemns, but understands. And because the two of you together see these unspeakable horrors, they are robbed of their over-whelming terror. Down and down, and when the bottom is reached, up and up and up to health and wholeness.

This is only a hint of what we have in Jesus. He has descended into hell. And so he can go with you into the abyss of your own private hell, whatever it is. He can plumb the abyss and rob it of its wordless terror. He can conquer the death that is in you. He can bring health and wholeness and life. I do not know what your private hell is, but I know it is not off bounds for him. In him that most precious word of the Old Testament becomes true: "If I make my bed in hell, behold, thou art there!" (Ps. 139:8, KJV).

Lord, we believe; help our unbelief!

18

The Third Day He Rose Again from The Dead

1 Corinthians 15:20–23
Luke 24:28–35

I approach this study with joy. So far, with the Apostles' Creed, our course has been downward into ever-deepening gloom. We have affirmed that God's only Son suffered the indignity of human birth "under circumstances of more than ordinary abasement," as the Larger Catechism says (Q. 47). He lived under the unpredictable arbitrariness of human political arrangements, where those in power see what justice is, until their own interests are involved. He died as a victim of torture and capital punishment. And then he descended into hell, experiencing the absence of God totally and absolutely. Now at last the creed takes an upward turn with the glad announcement, "The third day he rose again from the dead!"

I've always felt that when Christians reach this point in reciting the creed, they should make some kind of demonstration: the Nixon victory sign, or the black power salute, or the charismatic lifting of hands, or something. The least we can do is quicken the pace and increase the volume, to make a joyful noise unto the Lord. Bach does it best. If you have ever heard the Credo in the B-minor Mass, you surely remember it. *"Et sepulchrus est"*—and he was buried—ends with the wailing of strings, softer and softer until the sound dies in utter despair. There is a moment of silence so heavy it weighs you down. Then the director raises his baton, and all the timpani and all the trumpets and all the singers burst forth with *"Et resurrexit"*—and he rose again! We are at that throat-catching moment in the creed.

I

It is fashionable once again to talk of the return from death to life. For a good many years we have been hearing in lectures and seeing in print the stories of people who were clinically dead and have been resuscitated and brought back to life, and who have vivid memories of what the gates of death are like.

Guideposts magazine published an article by George G. Ritchie, M.D., who was pronounced dead of double lobar pneumonia at an army hospital in Texas in 1943. As his body was being prepared for the morgue, a medic thought he saw movement. The doctor was called back, he injected adrenaline into the heart, and George Ritchie lived to become a doctor and write his article. What he experienced in those moments was a complete disassociation from his body. He saw it dead, lying on the cot. He left and headed for Richmond, Virginia, where he wanted to enter medical school. But then he felt he had to turn around and reenter the hospital room. Again he saw the body and was overcome with despair. Then light filled the room. His total life passed in review before him. There was a presence in the room and he felt flooded, pierced, illuminated by compassion. He went to sleep and woke up later as a very sick but recovering patient in the hospital.

In the *Canadian Medical Association Journal* an article appeared entitled "Cardiac Arrest Remembered." The attending physician recorded the account of his patient in which he seemed to "float free" from the body, experiencing a great sense of well-being, while a pale yellow light filled the room.

This is fascinating material. It should be of comfort to those of us who dread the experience of death. I am not prepared to say that it furnishes scientific proof of life beyond death. Nor am I inclined to make any theological assertions on the basis of these kinds of data. I mention them because most of us have heard them and may be wondering how they relate to the resurrection of Jesus Christ. I think it may be very helpful for us to contrast the resurrection with this material, to show how different Jesus' resurrection is from even the most glorious of these stories.

II

For one thing, the victory over death in these resuscitation stories is temporary. No one doubts—neither the one who tells the story nor the one who hears it—that these people will eventually die. Death has been postponed for them as it was for many people in the Bible: the Shunammite widow's son whom Elisha raised, the widow of Nain's son and Jairus's daughter and Lazarus whom Jesus raised, Dorcas whom Peter raised—death has been postponed for them, but death has not been conquered.

But Christ being risen dies no more. In Christ's resurrection death is not postponed; it is overcome. Death is like a dragon whose back is broken. His tail still thrashes and we still suffer death, but we know that its awesome power is gone. "O death, where is thy victory? O death, where is thy sting? . . . Thanks be to God who gives us the victory through our Lord Jesus Christ" (1 Cor. 15:55, 57).

And that leads to the other distinction. Victory over death in these resuscitation stories is private and individual. The one who returns from the gates of death does not win a victory for anyone else.

But the resurrection is not just Christ's conquest of his own death. Once there was a man who died and came to life again; well, hooray for him? No! "As in Adam all die, so also in Christ shall all be made alive" (1 Cor. 15:22). The resurrection of Christ is the first fruits presaging and guaranteed the resurrection of us all. It has cosmic and corporate effects. It changes the odds. That wonderful phrase in the Nicene Creed, "for us . . . and for our salvation," governs not only Christ's birth and life and death on the cross and his harrowing of hell but also, and above all, his resurrection.

"A Declaration of Faith" expresses this truth as well as I can ever say it:

> In the death of Jesus Christ
>   God's way in the world seemed finally defeated.
> But death was no match for God.
> The resurrection of Jesus was God's victory over death. . . .
> We do not yet see the end of death.
> But Christ has been raised from the dead. . . .
> In his resurrection is the promise of ours. . . .
> So we treat death as a broken power.
> Its ultimate defeat is certain. . . .
> No life ends so tragically
>   that its meaning and value are destroyed.
> Nothing, not even death, can separate us
>   from the love of God in Jesus Christ our Lord.[15]

III

As we all know, the Bible contains some wonderful stories of how Jesus, after his victory over death, appeared to his disciples to instruct and reassure them. I am struck with the important part that eating plays in these stories.

My favorite is the story in Luke of the two who were walking on Easter evening to Emmaus. They did not recognize the stranger who joined them, but they invited him to supper. And when he blessed the bread and broke it and gave it to them, they recognized him.

Luke records that later that same night Jesus appeared to all the disciples and ate broiled fish with them. John has a long story of the breakfast Jesus served to the disciples after a night of fishing on the Sea of Galilee. And in Peter's sermon to Cornelius and his household, the punch line is that we "who were chosen by God as witnesses . . . ate and drank with him after he rose from the dead" (Acts 10:41).

I'm not sure what we are supposed to learn from these stories about the nature of the resurrection body and the kind of digestive system it has. The principal point is that

the risen Lord was eager to continue the complete sharing, the table fellowship, that he had had with his own all
during his ministry. He had shared their human lot completely: hunger, dependence on bread, fasting, feasting.
So now in these meals they share his victory over death.

This, dear friends, is the central meaning of the Lord's
Supper. The early church celebrated it on Sunday evening. Why? That's when the resurrection appearances
took place. They were in the upper room, with the door
shut, and then there he was in the midst of them, saying,
"Peace be with you. Let's eat together the victory meal!"

Many people have told me that the Lord's Supper is for
them a very sad occasion. It is a time to think of their sins
and unworthiness, a time to remember Jesus' death, a time
to sit huddled in the pew with a somber face. In the language of the day, communion is a "downer." Now there
is sadness at communion, inescapably. The broken body
and the shed blood are before us. But that sadness is
caught up in triumph. We eat the supper after the resurrection. It's a victory banquet! It's a *celebration* of the
defeat of death. Communion, properly understood and
properly celebrated—that's the word, celebrated—is an
"upper."

"The third day he rose again from the dead"—for us.
And we come to communion to meet him—alive again—
and to celebrate his victory.

Lord, we believe; help our unbelief.

19

He Ascended Into Heaven, and Sitteth on the Right Hand of God the Father Almighty

Acts 1:6–11

Now, in our series on the Apostles' Creed, we have come to the mouth-filling phrase, "He ascended into heaven, and sitteth on the right hand of God the Father Almighty." It's great to be on the upswing! For so long we were plunging down, down, down into the abyss: conceived, born, suffered, crucified, dead, buried, descended into hell. Finally, we started back up: "The third day he rose again from the dead." And now, with a rush, we are climbing to the heights, to the right hand of God the Father Almighty.

It's great to come to the present tense! For so long we've been rehearsing the past, but in this phrase we finally make an affirmation about what is happening today: he sitteth on the right hand of God the Father Almighty.

But for all our joy, we know we're in trouble. The words "ascended into heaven" cause us twentieth-century believers the same difficulty we encountered with the phrase "descended into hell." Let's try to deal with the difficulty first.

I

Many, many years ago when our twin sons were very small, I had to take a plane to attend a church meeting. They accompanied me to the airport and watched as my plane took off and went higher and higher until it was a tiny speck and then disappeared. When I came back they were there to meet me, and one of them reached out and rubbed my head. "Did it squeeze your head, Daddy?" he asked. What a revelation of how a child's mind works! He saw the plane growing smaller and smaller and figured it was squeezing his daddy tighter and tighter.

In his book *The Creed in Christian Teaching*, James Smart says, "Sunday schools have been known to use a series of slides to depict the ascension, the first showing Jesus hovering in the air just above the heads of his disciples, the second and third showing him smaller and smaller as he ascends in the air, and the fourth representing him as a tiny figure disappearing into the clouds of the sky. The visual aid was quite effective in impressing upon the minds of children a false and confusing conception of a spiritual reality."[16] I wonder how many of the children secretly thought his head was squeezed!

"He descended into hell . . . he ascended into heaven"—a three-story universe: earth in the middle, hell below, heaven above. How are we going to deal with that when we know the earth is not a fixed platform but a rotating, circling ball, so that all notions of above and below are strictly relative? Hell, that place of God's absence, of separation and alienation from God, of rebellion against God, is not literally down there somewhere in the core of planet earth. And heaven, that place of God's presence, of harmony and loving obedience, is not literally up there through space, not even beyond the farthest star.

Before we become too critical of the spatial language of the New Testament and the Apostles' Creed, let us admit that for all our vaunted scientific knowledge, we still talk in the terms of space because we can't find any other terms. I have often chuckled over Bishop John A. T. Robinson's bestseller of a few years back, *Honest to God*. The good bishop really poked fun at our traditional notions that God is "up there" or "out there." No, said the bishop, using some ideas of Paul Tillich, God is the ground of our being, God is found in the depth of human relationships.

This seemed to me to be a thinly veiled way of saying God is "down there," grounding everything, in the depths. As space-time creatures, we have to think of a reality markedly different from our world as another place.

Heaven is markedly different from the world we know. God's rule, God's control, God's kingdom, which are so hidden here, are evident and obvious there. God's will, which is so often violated here, is done perfectly and promptly and gladly there. Heaven is where God's throne is, the effective, central seat of God's loving power and powerful love. The real danger is not in speaking of this order of reality in spatial terms but in denying it altogether. For this is the order of reality into which Jesus has entered, with profound results for you and me.

II

One of the central questions faced by the apostles and early believers was, Where is Jesus now? They had no doubt about A.D. 1–30, his life in the flesh, all those verbs in the past tense that we confess in the creed. They were eyewitnesses and had seen and experienced those things. They had no doubt that they had seen him alive and eaten with him after his death—that final past tense, "The third day he rose again from the dead." But the postresurrection encounters ceased. At Pentecost the Holy Spirit came as the means and the fashion of Christ's continuing, powerful presence with his people. The author of the fourth Gospel understood clearly that the coming of the Holy Spirit was dependent on the going away of Jesus: "Nevertheless I tell you the truth: it is to your advantage that I go away, for if I do not go away, the Counselor will not come to you; but if I go, I will send him to you" (John 16:7). Where did Jesus go away to? That was the question.

For an answer, they searched the scriptures. The only scriptures they had were the books of the Old Testament. And the most familiar was the hymnbook, the book of Psalms. And in Psalm 110 they found their answer:

The LORD says to my lord:
"Sit at my right hand,
till I make your enemies your footstool."

Jesus the Lord is seated at God's right hand, the position
of supreme majesty and authority in the entire creation.
He sits there while God makes his enemies his footstool.
What an interesting way to understand all the centuries of
human history since the resurrection of Jesus, including
our own century right now! Those centuries are the long
process whereby, one by one, the enemies of Jesus are
unmasked, subdued, overthrown, and made a stool for his
feet.

You and I would expect Psalm 23 to be the most quoted
psalm in the New Testament. But Psalm 110 wins, hands
down. Jesus quotes it. Paul quotes it. Peter quotes it. "You
will see the Son of man seated at the right hand of Power,"
says Jesus (Mark 14:62). He is "exalted at the right hand of
God," says Peter in his sermon on the day of Pentecost
(Acts 2:33). "Behold, I see the heavens opened, and the
Son of man standing at the right hand of God," says Ste-
phen just before being stoned to death (Acts 7:56). "Who
is to condemn?" asks Paul. "Is it Christ Jesus, who died,
yes, who was raised from the dead, who is at the right hand
of God, who indeed intercedes for us?" (Rom. 8:34). The
first letter of Peter speaks of "Jesus Christ, who has gone
into heaven and is at the right hand of God, with angels,
authorities, and powers subject to him" (1 Peter 3:21–22).
And the writer to the Hebrews says, "When he had made
purification for sins, he sat down at the right hand of the
Majesty on high" (Heb. 1:3).

The actual story of the ascension, of the translation from
here to there, is told only in Luke 24 and Acts 1. I hope
that we are now prepared to see in it not the record of a
mission to outer space, complete with countdown and
blast-off, but a reverent attempt to say that the postresurrection appearances did cease and that the man Jesus is no
longer a part of our space-time reality but a part of ulti-

mate, final reality in the very throne room of God. Not that he has abandoned us. Through the Holy Spirit he keeps his promise to be with us always, to the end of the age—with us more intimately and universally than he could be even in the days of his flesh. But the thing we want to affirm about the man Jesus now, in the present tense, is that having ascended into heaven he sitteth—right now—on the right hand of God the Father Almighty.

III

So what? We can see easily enough that it makes a difference for the comfort and presence of Jesus to be available to us here on earth through the Holy Spirit. But what difference does it make that he himself in another realm of reality sits on the right hand of God?

In the first place, it makes a difference in how we understand *power.* Earlier in this book, we meditated on the phrase "suffered under Pontius Pilate." We said that Jesus was at the mercy of the same kind of political rulers who rule us and have always ruled the human race: men and women who can see justice clearly enough—until their own selfish interests are involved. But there is an unseen side to the power picture. In that markedly different realm of reality, in the throne room of God, the power is not in the hands of Pilate but in the hands of our risen and ascended Lord. He, the innocent sufferer, the victim, the lamb that opened not his mouth—he has the real and ultimate power, not at the end of time but right now in the present. This is the faith that has always given Christians a strange freedom in relation to political power, from the earliest days of the martyrs down to the Declaration of Barmen in our own time.

In the second place, it makes a difference in how we understand *prayer.* For what Christ is doing as he sits at God's right hand is making intercession for us. It means something to me that my weak, poorly formed, infrequent, and inadequate petitions are floated before God on the surface of an overflowing, mighty stream of prayer made for me and all others by my risen ascended Lord. He learned obedience through what he suffered. He prayed in the days of his flesh with loud cries and bloody sweat. He is not ashamed to call us brothers and sisters. He is touched with the feeling of our infirmities, for he has been tempted in all respects as we are tempted, yet without sin. And day and night he busies himself with his prayers for us and the few that we make for ourselves, offering them as a well-loved Son to his Father. If I could remember that, I might not lose heart so quickly in my praying. I might become what I have so long aspired to be, a person of prayer.

In the third place, it makes a difference in how we understand *God*. I remember how startled I was when I first heard the title of Karl Barth's beautiful little book, *The Humanity of God*. That's what the ascension is all about, the humanity of God. For Jesus carried our humanity into the throne room of God and into the innermost life of the Godhead. The adventure of the incarnation did not leave God unchanged. For now God knows what it's like to be human! "A Declaration of Faith" puts it this way:

> He lives as one of us with God.
> Because he shares our humanity
>   and has bound us to himself in love,
>   we have an advocate in the innermost life of God.[17]

The poet Robert Browning, who is also among the prophets, says it best. In the poem "Saul," young David, trying to comfort King Saul in his deep depression, is led out beyond himself to say:

> " 'Tis the weakness in strength, that I cry for! my flesh, that I seek
> In the Godhead! I seek and I find it. O Saul, it shall be
> A Face like my face that receives thee; a Man like to me,
> Thou shalt love and be loved by, forever: a Hand like this hand
> Shall throw open the gates of new life to thee!
>   See the Christ stand!"[18]

He, our brother, ascended into heaven and sitteth on the right hand of God the Father Almighty. Because of that, power is different, and prayer is different, and even God is different!

20

From Thence He Shall Come to Judge the Quick and the Dead

Romans 2:1–16

The second article of the Apostles' Creed has to do with Jesus Christ. It is the longest article and forms the heart of the creed. We come at last to its final phrase: "From thence he shall come to judge the quick and the dead."

We recall that the second article begins with a series of past tenses: conceived, born, suffered, crucified, dead, buried, descended, rose, ascended. Then came a glorious present tense: "sitteth on the right hand of God the Father Almighty." And now comes a future tense: "shall come to judge the quick and the dead."

I

Jesus Christ has a future! That's the tremendous thing we say at this point in the creed. He is not just a great figure of the past like Plato, or Confucius, or Muhammad, or Caesar, or Napoleon, or Thomas Jefferson. The world has not seen the last of Jesus! We shall encounter him again at the end of human history. He will not sit forever in heaven, waiting for his enemies to be made his footstool. He shall come to judge the quick and the dead!

A brief word about that Elizabethan English. "Quick" is an old expression for "living, alive." It has some relevance in the twentieth century. One of my friends says that when the light turns to WALK at a busy intersection, you'd better be quick if you don't want to be dead. The creed's point is that the future of Jesus Christ does not involve a single generation, the generation living at the end of history. It involves all generations, including our own. Even if we are dead, we will be involved in that final encounter with Jesus Christ and with his final judgment.

There are two kinds of churches. There are churches where we hear nothing except the second coming of Jesus Christ. Charts and diagrams of history's final drama are the center of attention. Debates concern the exact sequence of the appearance of the antichrist, the great tribulation, the rapture, the millennium, and the second death. Such churches seem to have given up on this world and its problems, to have abandoned the mass of humankind in order to form a close-knit society of potential escapees. The other kind of church is one where we never hear about the second coming at all. We are concerned with all sorts of proximate hopes: a full sanctuary, a balanced budget for next year, a complete slate of church school teachers; or control of inflation, peace in the Middle East, an end to racism. And these hopes tend to replace any overarching hope for the kingdom of God.

It is good for all churches of the second kind to stand and say in the creed, "From thence he shall come to judge the quick and the dead."

II

In the future of Jesus Christ there is bad news and there is good news. Which would you like to hear first?

The bad news is that there really will be a judgment. As Romans 2:16 puts it, there will be a day when God judges the secrets of men and women by Christ Jesus. Unlike even our best human judgments, God's judgment will be based on total truth. We try to reach "the truth, the whole truth, and nothing but the truth," but of course we never arrive. Much remains secret. We have to do the best we can with the partial, conflicting evidence we get from our witnesses. But at the end, finally, truth will out. There will be no secrets.

The picture of this judgment in the book of Revelation is dramatic and terrifying: "Then I saw a great white throne and him who sat upon it; from his presence earth and sky fled away, and no place was found for them. And I saw the dead, great and small, standing before the throne, and the books were opened" (20:11-12).

All the truth is in those books. Not the image you tried carefully to project, but what you really were underneath. Not the kind words you didn't mean, but the hostility you really felt. All the deceitful games you played with people. All the secret ways in which you manipulated others to do what you wanted. All the frauds and deceits you practiced on yourself. There will be no need for a Freedom of Information Act when those books are opened; you can keep nothing back as a threat to national security. The plain, unvarnished, total truth about you and about everybody else will be revealed.

The result of total truth will be absolutely devastating. Pascal said that if people could know what was said about them in secret, there would not be two friends in the world. And if men and women could know what they really look like in the light of absolute truth, there would not be one self-righteous person left. In that day we will pronounce the verdict on ourselves—"Guilty." "All have sinned and fall short of the glory of God" (Rom. 3:23). "None is righteous, no, not one" (Rom. 3:10).

Even the bad news has a good side, if we move beyond our immediate self-interest. Would you want deceit and lies and games to be eternal, to go on forever? Even if it embarrasses, humiliates, and devastates us, there is something good about the hope that truth will out, that finally the facts will be manifest, that everyone will agree at last: "That's right; that's the way it was and is."

III

But there is positive good news. In our reading from
Romans, Paul calls the future in which God will judge the
secrets of men and women part of his "gospel," part of the
good news he has to declare. The reason it is good news
is that God will judge those secrets "by Jesus Christ." Jesus
Christ will be our judge, not Pontius Pilate, who can be
blinded by self-interest, not even the best and wisest of our
human judges, and not a divine Judge who does not know
what it's like to be human, but Jesus Christ himself.

He will pronounce the sentence. As we have said, there
will be no question about the facts and we will all plead
guilty. But in his sentencing our Judge will be full of compassion. It is interesting to me that scripture says two
things about the sentencing. Many passages seem to say all
will be pardoned. Many other passages speak of a sharp
division between the right hand and the left, the sheep
and the goats. This ought to make us very modest in our
conjectures about what sentence will be passed on those
who are not Christians or who never had the chance to be
Christians. Rather let us rejoice in the totally undeserved
good news that comes to us who believe. Here is how the
Heidelberg Catechism puts it:

> Q. 52. What comfort does the return of Christ "to judge
> the living and and the dead" give you?
> That in all affliction and persecution I may await with
> head held high the very Judge from heaven who has already
> submitted himself to the judgment of God for me and has
> removed all the curse from me.

But the Judge will do more than pronounce the sentence:
he will set things right. When God comes to judge the
fatherless and the widow in the Old Testament, God does
not come to sentence them but to see that they get justice.
So in the last judgment, the Judge will restore and relieve
the victims of crime and injustice. And because injustice
is systemic, built into our human systems, the Judge will

renew all things and create new heavens and a new earth in which righteousness dwells. Here is how "A Declaration of Faith" puts it:

All things will be renewed in Christ. . . .
As he stands at the center of our history,
    we are confident he will stand at its end.
He will judge all people and nations.
Evil will be condemned
    and rooted out of God's good creation.
There will be no more tears or pain.
All things will be made new.
The fellowship of human beings with God and each other
    will be perfected.[19]

IV

Once again we raise the question, So what? How does it affect our lives here and now to believe that "from thence he shall come to judge the quick and the dead"? The Marxists claim that such religion is an opiate of the people. We train people to sit down and do nothing about the injustices in the world because they hope for "pie in the sky by and by." But the effect can be just the opposite. There is such a thing as an ethic of anticipation. Since this is the way it is going to be ultimately and finally, let us begin now. Let us tell the truth now. Let us stop playing games with each other now. If we are to be judged by how we have treated the least of these, Christ's brothers and sisters, let us begin now to reevaluate who's important. Let us approximate justice. Let us practice compassion. Let us stop worrying so much about what people think and what people may say and what the newspaper may publish. Let us ask what the Judge will think and what the Judge will say.

A friend of mine was a pastor in South Carolina at the height of the civil rights struggle. One of his members came to him, very upset, to ask why he preached so much about justice to black people. "Because," my friend told him, "I believe in the last judgment. In that day you will know the truth. You will understand clearly that the way you treat powerless people is the way you treat Jesus Christ himself. And when all that hits you, I don't want you to look across at me, your pastor, and ask, 'Why didn't you tell me?' I want to be clear of your blood." "Do you really believe in the last judgment?" said the man. "Literally," said my friend.

21

I Believe
in the Holy Ghost

Ezekiel 37
John 3:1–12

We have arrived at the third article of the Apostles' Creed. First article: God the Father; second article: Jesus Christ, God's only Son; third article: the Holy Ghost. We recognize immediately that we are in the presence of the three "persons" of the Trinity. We don't discuss the Trinity much in church these days, but we do sing about it: "God in three persons, blessed Trinity."

Although the creed is trinitarian in form, it does not wrestle with what really constitutes a "doctrine" of the Trinity: the unity of, and the distinctions between, the three persons. Like scripture it poses the riddle: How can these three be only one God? And like scripture it does not attempt an answer. That is left for the Nicene Creed and particularly the Athanasian Creed.

The third person is clearly the most mysterious person of the Trinity. One thing that contributes to the mystery is the Elizabethan word "ghost." When I was a child I had mental pictures of a thing in bedsheets that went bump in the night. I know now that is not what "Holy Ghost" means. It simply means "Holy Spirit."

That doesn't help very much, because of all the words that are hard to define, that are difficult for the modern mind to wrap itself around, "spirit" is near the top of the list. We are not clear what we mean by "team spirit" or "the spirit of the times" or "the human spirit." And we are even less clear what we mean by "the Holy Spirit" or "the Spirit of God."

We don't know what pronouns to use. The Old Testament word for spirit is feminine. The New Testament word for spirit is neuter. The special word for spirit in John—*paraclete*—is masculine.

We can't draw a picture of the Holy Spirit. Artists have dared to picture the Father. The Son has a paintable human form. But we have only symbols for the Holy Spirit: the flame of fire or the dove. Professor Joseph Haroutunian of McCormick Seminary used to open his lectures on the Holy Spirit with something like this: "Most people when they think about the Trinity think of the Father, the Son, and the Pigeon. Now the Father is the Father of the Son, and the Son is the Son of the Father, but *who* is the Holy Ghost?" Who indeed?

We find ourselves in the position of Nicodemus in John 3. When Jesus started talking about the Spirit, Nicodemus got lost. But if we listen closely we will hear Jesus telling him what the Spirit does, what the Spirit is like, and what the Spirit is unlike.

I

First, what does the Holy Spirit do? The Spirit brings about the new birth. Jesus tells Nicodemus that those who can see the kingdom of God are those who have been born of the Spirit. Nicodemus, with his literal mind, can think only of a second physical birth. But there is another kind of birth, another upsurge of life in all its newness and wonder, and the Spirit is the power of this birth. You may recall that the creed speaks earlier of Jesus as "conceived by the Holy Ghost," and we spoke then of a spiritual life that may be conceived in us by the same Spirit.

When Paul writes of what the Spirit does, he uses, instead of birth, the symbol of resurrection. "If the Spirit of him who raised Jesus from the dead dwells in you, he who raised Christ Jesus from the dead will give life to your mortal bodies also through his Spirit which dwells in you" (Rom. 8:11).

Both birth and resurrection have to do with *new life*.

Once we have seen this clue, almost everywhere we look in the Bible there is a tie between the Spirit and life. In Ezekiel's famous vision of the valley of dry bones, it is when the Spirit enters into the lifeless corpses of the Hebrew nation that they stand up on their feet, an exceedingly great host. "I will put my Spirit within you," says the Lord, "and you shall live" (Ezek. 37:14). Jesus, as pictured in the fourth Gospel, speaks the same way: "It is the spirit that gives life, the flesh is of no avail; the words that I have spoken to you are spirit and life" (John 6:63). And one of Paul's favorite contrasts is between the written code that kills and the Spirit who gives life (Rom. 7:6; 2 Cor. 3:6). Thus, in the Nicene Creed we confess our faith in the Spirit, "the Lord and Giver of Life." And in a familiar hymn we sing, "Breathe on me, Breath of God, fill me with life anew."

Whenever there comes into your life and mine a genuine moment of renewal—not a forced reform, not a good resolution springing from our own tortured effort, not a gritting of the teeth and a tugging at our own bootstraps, but a gracious renewal from a power beyond ourselves, a new birth, a resurrection, a new creation—there the Spirit has been at work.

This is possibly seen more clearly corporately than individually. By all rights the Christian church should have died long ago. Again and again the church has abandoned its first love, become neither cold nor hot, grown encrusted with dead forms, burdened with hardened institutions, disgraced by the sinfulness of those who hold power within it, conformed to the image of this world. But just when from every human point of view the church is dead beyond recall, a strange power of renewal sets to work in the very bosom of that dead institution. From within the church God raises up an Anthony, a Francis of Assisi, a Martin Luther, a John Wesley, a William Carey, a John the

Twenty-third. And if we have eyes to see it, there the inexplicable miracle is!

II

Now, what is the Holy Spirit like? The Spirit is like the wind. In fact, the word for wind is the same as the word for spirit in both Hebrew and Greek. Jesus was using a gentle pun with Nicodemus. The wind seems very ordinary to most of us city dwellers. We seldom think about it until it blows down our power lines, depriving us of our television programs. But in Palestine, the wind makes all the difference. If it blows from the east, off the desert, it scorches the crops, dries out the nostrils, sometimes buries a village in burning sand. "A hot wind, off the bare heights" was the prophetic description of disaster and destruction. If it blows from the west, off the great sea, it brings rain to a parched land, renewing life. Life depends on how the wind blows. Yet you cannot make it blow. You cannot command it or summon it. It blows when it gets ready. And when it blows, you cannot see it. You can only hear its sound. Mysterious, invisible, uncontrollable, life-blasting or life-giving power—this is what the Spirit is like.

III

Now, what is the Spirit unlike? The flesh. That which is born of the flesh is flesh and that which is born of the Spirit is spirit. "Flesh" is one of the key words of the New Testament and we need to handle it with care. Only rarely does it mean the soft parts of the human body, the meat on our bones. Life "in the flesh" is life where our human willing and desiring initiates and controls. Life in the Spirit is life where God's willing initiates and controls. So a fleshly birth is one initiated by the will of human beings. A spiritual birth is an upsurge of new life initiated by the will and purpose of God. The works of the flesh are our own efforts, done when and as and how we will. The fruits of the Spirit are God's initiatives taking place within us when and as and how God wills.

It is not easy to distinguish the Spirit from the flesh. We may think we are being moved by the Spirit of God when we are really following our own selfish desires. In the Old Testament the false prophets far outnumber the true ones: those who took the initiative and made themselves prophets outnumber those who were filled with the Spirit of God. In the New Testament the Spirit gives pastors and teachers to the church, but there are those who make themselves pastors and teachers. The Spirit gives tongues and healing and other gifts. But human desire and ambition—the flesh—can counterfeit the gifts of the Spirit.

How careful we need to be to distinguish between the Holy Spirit and its very opposite, the flesh! How often we must ask ourselves, Is this activity in which I think I am moved by the Holy Spirit really a form of self-seeking? Am I moved by my own selfish desires? Am I attracting people to myself, binding them to *me?* (Someone has said that if you remove the final *h* of *flesh* and then spell it backwards, you get *self!*) Am I manipulating other people? Am I seeking the glory that comes from them rather than the glory that comes from God? Am I waiting on God or plunging ahead on my own? That which is born of the flesh is flesh and that which is born of the Spirit is spirit.

What do we mean when we talk about "the Holy Spirit"? We mean the power of renewal, of new life, which is not our own effort, not even the sum of our pooled human power, a power we cannot control or summon, that works when and as and how God wills, not as we will.

Let us admit that we have produced no picture of the Holy Spirit. The Spirit has no face. Perhaps one reason is that the Spirit is self-effacing. The Spirit bears witness not to itself but to Christ. The Spirit points away from itself to Christ. The Spirit is not an independent revelation of God. The Spirit is utterly subservient to the one revelation in the face of Jesus.

But if we cannot see the Spirit's face, we can, sometimes

unmistakably, recognize the Spirit's effects. As Jesus said, we can hear the sound thereof.

When my children were small, I was writing a dissertation on the Holy Spirit. You can imagine my difficulties when four little people kept asking, "Daddy, what *is* the Holy Spirit?" We were living in Alabama, in the fifties, and a great riot broke out in our town, protesting the integration of the University of Alabama. Our pastor was a very shy, retiring man. But that Sunday when he entered the pulpit there was something different about him. With a power that none of us had ever seen before, he laid his job on the line—indeed, his life on the line—to tell us clearly and unmistakably that every single human being, regardless of color, is precious in the sight of God. There was a great stillness. New people were being born. Even my children were quiet. In the car on the way home I said quietly, "Now I think you know what the Holy Spirit is." And they nodded.

22

The Holy Catholic Church

1 Corinthians 1:1–3

Before we continue with the remaining phrases in the third article of the creed, we need to face an interesting question: Is the entire third article about the Holy Spirit, just as the whole second article is about Jesus Christ? The case can be made that it is. If we had time we could quote scripture to show that the Spirit identifies and empowers *the church;* that the Spirit creates and sustains the common life, the *communion of the saints;* that the Spirit engenders in our hearts the faith by which we grasp and accept the *forgiveness of sins;* that the Spirit is the *resurrection* power; that the Spirit is the power of the age to come, of the *life everlasting.*

It is evident, however, that each of these phrases in the third article can stand on its own feet, is important enough to merit attention in its own right. There are some basic things that we believe in addition to the three persons of the Trinity. And the first one that the creed suggests is "the holy catholic church."

When we reach this point, we come down with a thud, like a hang glider who after hours in the air loses momentum and crashes to earth. All this time we've been way up there with the Father, whom no one has ever seen; and the Son, whom people once saw but who is now out of sight, ascended into heaven, sitting on the right hand of God; and the Holy Ghost, windlike, powerful, uncontrollable, invisible. And then—*thud!*—the church, earthbound, housed in buildings, supported by budgets, run by committees, a very human, visible, concrete institution.

Well, you say, at least it's easier to believe in the church than in all that preceding business about creation and spiritual conception and virgin birth and descent into hell and ascent into heaven. At least I can get my hands on the church, see it, smell it, praise it, damn it, join it, leave it. It's here!

Yes, indeed it's here. Dietrich Bonhoeffer never tired of saying, "The church takes up space on earth." If to believe means to admit the existence of, we all believe in the church with no difficulty. It obviously exists. But if to believe means, as we said at the outset, to put your trust in, we may have reached the most difficult article in the creed.

How many of us have some complaint to make against the church? How many of us have been sorely disillusioned by the church?

Passing over matters that might be petty and personal, let us face the obvious fact that the church is an institution. Many of us have great hesitation about putting any kind of trust in institutions. Institutions always harden and petrify the living idea they are supposed to preserve and spread. Institutions become increasingly inefficient. They develop bureaucracies, and many of us recognize bureaucracy as the ultimate enemy. Institutions are subject to Parkinson's Law: work multiplies to fill the time available; staffs increase regardless of the work to be done. Institutions are subject to the Peter Principle: people are advanced until they reach their level of incompetence. It would be funny if it were not so true.

Can the creed really be serious in asking you to put your trust in the church? If it is, we need to think through this article with great care.

I

The first thing we are asked to believe is that the church is holy. Does this mean the church is without error and without sin? You know better than that. The church is an association of sinners; in fact that's the entrance requirement. The first question we ask new members in the Presbyterian Church is: "Do you acknowledge yourself to be a sinner in the sight of God?" You could just as easily get into Alcoholics Anonymous without being an alcoholic as you can get into the church without being a sinner. It's true that AA members are working on their addiction and church members are working on their sinfulness, but you are bound to find drunks in AA and you are bound to find sinners in the church. Corporately the church has done stupid things, like condemning Galileo for teaching that the earth revolves. It has done immoral things, like blessing slavery. It has done cruel things, like persecuting the Jews. Some of the horrible pages of history concern the cruelty of Catholics to Protestants and of Protestants to Catholics and of both to the Anabaptists and other groups on the left wing of the Reformation. Obviously when we say we believe in the holy church we cannot mean we believe in an infallible and sinless church.

Perhaps what we mean is that the church is at least a bit better than the rest of humanity. The church shares in human sinfulness, but not as deeply. There are, to be sure, fine people in the church, and I thank God for every one of them. But what are we going to do with the familiar "problem" of "the good humanist"? Don't we know men and women who are not members of any church, who make no profession of religion at all, yet are as kind, honest, generous, and courageous in all good causes as exemplary church members? The answer is yes, I do know such people, and I thank God for them, too.

What has been my lifelong agony about the church is its slowness to take the lead in all the great moral struggles of our day. Despite the number of fine people in it, the church so often brings up the rear, with a very nonheroic "me too," toward the very end of the parade. When we say we believe in the holy church we cannot mean we believe in a church that is obviously more compassionate and just than many who are outside of it.

Holy means "belonging to God, set apart for God, chosen by God for a special function." Jerusalem was Israel's holy city: not the biggest city, or the most prosperous city, or the most righteous city, but the place where God chose to put the divine name. Israel was a holy people: not the strongest nation, or the most populous, or the most attractive, or the most righteous, but the people on whom God had chosen to put the divine name and through whom God had chosen to carry out the divine purposes. So when we say the church is holy, we mean that this particular group of people, sometimes difficult and ornery people, are those on whom God chooses to put the divine name and through whom God proposes to work in a special way.

God really tests our faith by saying to us, If you want to approach me, to make contact with me, to be filled with my Spirit, you've got to meet me in this unlikely, fallible, sinful group of people, who are organized into this divided, often stupid, always sinful and imperfect institution.

This demand is so tough that the history of Christian theology is full of attempts to weasel out. The most famous is the double theology of the invisible church and the visible church. The visible church, so we are taught, is full of hypocrites, mired in institutional machinery, divided into denominations and factions. But the invisible church is known only to God; it contains only the genuinely converted; it is not earthbound or institutionalized or divided. There is some truth here, as we shall see, but it can be a terrible dodge: I don't have to try to overcome the divisions in the church, because the invisible church is not divided; I don't have to love the hypocrites about me because they probably are not members of the invisible church.

No, this visible, fallible, sinful institution is the only church there is. As Karl Barth wrote, "Take good note,

that a parson who does not believe that in this congregation of his, including those men and women, old wives and
children, Christ's congregation exists, does not believe at
all in the existence of the church!"[20]

But the visible church does have hidden dimensions we
do not easily see. Behind its fallibility and sinfulness there
is something else. In C. S. Lewis's *Screwtape Letters,* the
demon Screwtape writes to his nephew Wormwood, who
is charged with bringing his patient, a new Christian,
safely home to hell. Don't ever let him see the church as
we tremblingly see her, he says, "spread out through all
time and space and rooted in eternity, terrible as an army
with banners."[21] That is what God sees in the depths of the
visible church. And that is what we affirm when we say, "I
put my trust in the holy church."

II

The creed also says that the church is catholic. This
causes problems to Protestants because if they look up
Catholic Church in the telephone book, they run into a
highly visible institution: the Roman Catholic Church with
its diocesan offices, its bishop, its pope, its mass and confes-
sional and so on—the very church from which their ancestors broke away more than four hundred years ago. Why
should Protestants say, Sunday after Sunday, "I believe in
the holy catholic church"?

Because the word "catholic," with a little *c,* simply
means universal, found in all nations, not confined to one
nation. When God's people was simply the Jewish nation,
the church was not catholic. But when, under the gospel,
people of all nations, races, and languages came into the
people of God, then we had a catholic church.

We say in the creed that we put our trust in that kind
of church. We do not put our trust in a national church. We
do not put our trust in an "only true church" that denies
the name of Christian to all who do not wear one special
label. We do not put our trust in a racist church that includes only one race of people. The church by very defini-

tion is catholic, worldwide, multinational, multiracial. The Westminster Confession is very clear on this point: "The visible Church, which is also catholic or universal under the gospel (not confined to one nation as before under the law), consists of all those throughout the world that profess the true religion, together with their children" (6.141).

> We thank Thee that Thy Church unsleeping,
> While earth rolls onward into light,
> Through all the world her watch is keeping,
> And rests not now by day or night.
>
> As o'er each continent and island
> The dawn leads on another day,
> The voice of prayer is never silent,
> Nor dies the strain of praise away.[22]

That's what we affirm when we say, "I believe in the holy catholic church."

III

Many, many years ago, Paul called in his secretary, a man named Sosthenes, and said, "Take a letter to the church at Corinth." Then he paused for a long time, while Sosthenes held his pen over the parchment, ready to write. What a sorry church it was! It was split into four warring factions. Its members were not famous or well born. They were so unspiritual they could not comprehend any meaty theology. Yet they thought they were wise and felt qualified to judge and condemn Paul! One of the prominent members was living out of wedlock with his own stepmother. They were suing each other in the pagan courts. Some were libertines who claimed that the freedom with which Christ had set them free made it all right for them to indulge in sexual license, thievery, greed, drunkenness, even idolatry. At the Lord's Supper, some got drunk and others went hungry. The charismatic movement had broken out, and their services of worship were utter confusion in which all tried to speak at once in unknown tongues. Some were teaching that there is no resurrection. And they were behind on the every-member canvass! It was Paul's job to write in response to all those problems. He took a deep breath and began to dictate:

"Paul, called by the will of God to be an apostle of Christ Jesus, and our brother Sosthenes, To the church of God which is at Corinth, to those sanctified [made holy] in Christ Jesus [the holy church!], called to be saints [holy people] together with all those who in every place call on the name of our Lord Jesus Christ, both their Lord and ours [the catholic church!]: Grace to you and peace from God our Father and the Lord Jesus Christ" (1 Cor. 1:1–3).

It's all there, isn't it? Paul could see, behind the shabby outward appearance of the church at Corinth, the church of God that is spread out through all time and space and rooted in eternity, terrible as an army with banners. Paul could look at that church and still believe in the holy catholic church.

Lord, we believe; help our unbelief!

23

The Communion of Saints

John 15:4–5
Acts 4:32–35

What picture forms in your mind when you hear the phrase "the communion of saints"? A communion service? And around the table saints Peter and Paul and Augustine and Teresa and Agnes and the others, all with halos around their heads—and the whole thing framed in a beautiful stained glass window?

That picture is not all wrong. In many churches the communion liturgy contains words like these: "Many will come from east and west, and from north and south, and sit at table with Abraham, Isaac, and Jacob in the kingdom of God." Communion celebrates that future great feast in the kingdom when all those great saints of the past will be gathered together. The familiar anthem of the New Orleans Jazz Funeral catches up the whole idea: "O when the saints come marching in, O when the saints come marching in, O Lord, I want to be in that number, when the saints come marching in." The communion prayer often contains words like these: "With the church through all ages, we thank you for your saving love in Jesus Christ our Lord." Here and now the saints of the past commune with us. We are surrounded at the Lord's Table by a great cloud of witnesses. The picture of the saints—halos and all— around the communion table has great meaning for us whenever we celebrate the Lord's Supper.

I

But the phrase "the communion of saints" has a far wider meaning. Let's talk first about saints. The word "saint" ought not to be confined to those persons of exceptional piety and great devotion whom the Roman Catholic Church has officially canonized—the ones with the halos in the stained glass windows.

Several years ago I arrived at the church one morning to find our custodial staff in great excitement. They had discovered a woman sleeping in one of the pews in our sanctuary. How she got in they did not know, and I still do not know. When she woke up and got herself together she came around to my study and explained to me that she was an authentic saint. "My name," she said, "is St. Jane Jane." We smile at her eccentricity, but her terminology was right in line with the New Testament, for in the New Testament every believer, every Christian, every member of the church is a saint.

Earlier I said that the holiness of the church does not mean that this bumbling, bureaucratic institution is without error or without sin, or even better than other institutions. It just means that it is set apart, chosen by God, to help fulfill God's purposes in the world. Just so, a saint or holy person is not free from sin or better than the good humanists who profess no religion. But we are God's ungainly, awkward, chosen instruments, and so the most unlikely one of us is still a saint.

II

Now let's talk about communion. The word "communion" also has a wider range of meaning than we may have realized. It is related to our word "common"—having things in common, caring and sharing, swapping and exchanging. It indicates our fellowship or partnership in helping to fulfill the purposes of God.

When Jesus says, "Abide in me, and I in you," that's communion, a kind of mutual indwelling. Jesus uses the vine and the branches as an illustration. The vine fulfills its purpose, to bear fruit, through the branches; the whole vine pours itself into the branches. But the branches must also be in the vine, drawing their whole strength from the vine, else there will be no fruit. "For apart from me you can do nothing."

Many years ago, when I began work in my first parish, I remember I copied that text out and put it on my desk. So when I sat down to write a sermon or to plan my work, and when I got up to go visit my people up and down the country roads, I would see those words, "Apart from me you can do nothing." I need to do that again.

Now because saints have that kind of communion with Christ, they also have communion with one another. In the Acts of the Apostles the communion of saints is described again and again. "The company of those who believed," we read, "were of one heart and soul"—that's a communion of spirit, of desire, of purpose, of faith and love—"and no one said that any of the things which he possessed was his own, but they had everything in common"—that's communion of material things: money, land, houses, food. Someone has said that when your first child is born, the child's first word is "Da-da" or "Ma-ma." But the first word of the second child is "Mine!" In the communion of saints we get beyond that.

The word "communism" is close to our word "communion." The question is often raised whether the sharing of goods in the early church was a sort of primitive communism. There is, it seems to me, a very simple but decisive distinction between the two. Communism is a forced sharing. The state says to you, "What is yours is mine!" Communion is a voluntary sharing. One brother or sister says to another, "What is mine is yours!"

III

The best commentary I know on "the communion of saints" is in the Westminster Confession (6.146–147), and it is worth quoting extensively:

1. All saints being united to Jesus Christ their head, by his Spirit and by faith, have fellowship with him in his graces, sufferings, death, resurrection, and glory: and, being united to one another in love, they have communion in each other's gifts and graces, and are obliged to the performance of such duties, public and private, as do conduce to their mutual good. . . .

2. Saints by their profession are bound to maintain an holy fellowship and communion in the worship of God, and in performing such other spiritual services as tend to their mutual edification; as also in relieving each other in outward things, according to their several abilities and necessities. Which communion, as God offereth opportunity, is to be extended unto all those who, in every place, call upon the name of the Lord Jesus.

What we need to do is to extend this great chapter horizontally, moving out even beyond "all those who, in every place, call upon the name of the Lord Jesus" to the whole world, with whom we share common humanity, a common Creator, and a common Savior, though many have not accepted him yet. We have some kind of communion with everyone for whom Christ died. And if I understand John 3:16 correctly—"God so loved the world"— that's everybody on the face of the earth.

The communion of saints may begin with the communion plate, but it is not complete until it reaches the offering plate. The New Testament contains the record of a great offering, and twice it uses the word "communion" to describe that offering. It was the offering Paul took up among his Gentile converts for the relief of the saints at Jerusalem, who had suffered famine. The saints at Jerusalem had harassed and criticized the Gentile Christians. They had subverted Paul's churches, attacked his ministry, spread the rumor that he was a false apostle. Their theology was very questionable. But the offering was given sacrificially and turned over to them, even though Paul was arrested in the process. That's what's involved in saying with risk and passion, "I put my trust in the communion of saints!"

We have three chances to confess our faith in the communion of saints. One is when we stand to say the creed. One is when bread and wine are shared. And one is when the offering plate is passed.

Lord, we believe; help our unbelief!

24

The Forgiveness of Sins

Psalm 51
Matthew 6:14–15
Ephesians 4:31–32

"I believe in the forgiveness of sins." Behind us are fourteen chapters on phrases from the Apostles' Creed. We have made our way through the first article, "God the Father Almighty," and the second article, "Jesus Christ his only Son our Lord." And we have moved into the third article, "the Holy Ghost, the holy catholic church, the communion of saints." Now we finally arrive at what concerns us most closely, intimately, and personally: "I believe in the forgiveness of sins."

I

There's not a lot of forgiveness out there, is there? I know children who cannot forgive their parents and parents who cannot forgive their children. I know wives who cannot forgive their husbands and husbands who cannot forgive their wives. Arabs have difficulty forgiving Jews; and Jews, Arabs. Landlords and tenants. Borrowers and lenders. Competitors and competitors—not much forgiveness anywhere.

There are lots of substitutes around. As we saw in chapter 7, condoning is a substitute. "There, there, what you've done doesn't really matter. Don't mention it. Boys will be boys. It's all right. Forget it." Giving an offense the back of the hand is not forgiveness. It doesn't redeem the offender. It really puts down the offender, cheapens her or him. The offended one retains a position of vast superiority: "You can't really hurt me, even if you try."

Submission is another fake form of forgiveness. "OK, kick me again if it gives you so much pleasure. Go ahead. Make me suffer." Giving in is not forgiveness. The persecutor-victim model characterizes an amazing number of human relationships, between couples, between parent and child, between friend and friend. But it is not a redemptive pattern. Years of being the uncomplaining victim will not redeem the persecutor. All too often the offended one nurses hidden, unspoken anger and self-pity that thwart and stunt his or her own life.

Obtaining redress is a substitute. "Make up for what you have done, pay the damages, and we'll call it square." Giving up further claims when you have received a payoff for the offense you have suffered is not forgiveness. It does not redeem the offender. The offended one really gives nothing, for he or she is adequately recompensed. The books are balanced, but the people are essentially unchanged.

There is some real forgiveness out there somewhere. You and I have seen it and experienced it. That's how we can believe in it. "I was wrong and I know it. There's no way I can ever really make up for it." "Yes, you were wrong and it hurt me terribly. But you don't have to balance the books. I accept you and the pain you've caused me. I forgive you." Both parties are vulnerable, both suffer, and out of the pain comes a new relationship between them; forgiveness has been given and accepted.

Listen to the requests in Psalm 51: "have mercy on me . . . blot out my transgressions . . . wash me . . . cleanse me . . . teach me . . . purge me . . . fill me with joy . . . hide thy face from my sins . . . create in me a clean heart . . . put a new and right spirit within me . . . cast me not away . . . restore . . . uphold . . . deliver."

Forgiveness is a unique transaction. Vengeance strikes a chord in the human heart. We can read *The Count of Monte Cristo* and lick our lips as the hero gets even one by one with those who treated him unjustly. But what do we do with that strange story where an innocent man looks down from a cross into the faces of his persecutors and says, "Father, forgive them; they know not what they do"? Evenhanded justice we can understand and argue. Forgiveness transcends understanding and is above argument. The old saying is true: To err is human; to forgive, divine.

II

This unique transaction is far and away the most important thing that happens at church. The article, "I believe in the forgiveness of sins," is not an anticlimax in the creed; it is, in a way, the point the whole creed has been leading up to. The creation and governance of the world sets the stage for the career of Jesus Christ: conceived, born, suffered, crucified, buried, raised, ascended, seated. And the career of Jesus Christ sets the stage for the outpouring of the Holy Spirit. And the Holy Spirit creates here among us in our own history the holy catholic church, the communion of saints. And what happens in the church? The forgiveness of sins!

Why do we go to church? To hear the sermon? To listen to music? To honor our ancestors? To see the people? To give our money? To serve the community? To sing praises? To ask petitions? For all those and many other reasons.

But if the creed is right, there are two moments in the liturgy that transcend all others in importance. One is when the minister says, "Friends, believe the good news of the gospel. In Jesus Christ, we are forgiven!" In that moment we receive the forgiveness of God.

Do we really receive it, or is it an empty form? The test is whether we forgive ourselves. Many of us don't. We think we can say, in our heads, "Yes, God forgives me. I've been taught that since I was a child." But down in our viscera we can continue to accuse ourselves, continue to hold up for ourselves impossible and perfectionist expectations, continue to wallow in guilt because we don't come up to those expectations.

Unwillingness to forgive oneself is one of the signs of depression, that widespread disease from which most of us suffer at one time or another. Martin Luther had periodic bouts with severe depression. How ironic that the great Reformer, who made the forgiveness of sins central in his theology, the article by which the church stands or falls, should have had times in his life when he could not accept his own forgiveness! In good medieval fashion, Luther attributed those periods of depression and self-accusation to the devil. Once he was so prostrated that he could not raise his head, but scrawled with his finger the Latin words *baptizatus sum*—"I have been baptized." Wise Luther! For when our minds cannot hear or grasp the word of God's forgiveness, God has given us a sign on our bodies, the mark of baptism, the outward, visible, physical seal of his promise to accept us, to include us, to wash us, to forgive us. When we can no longer hear and believe words, baptism says to us viscerally, "Friends, believe the good news of the gospel. In Jesus Christ we are forgiven!"

The second transcendent moment in the liturgy is in the Lord's Prayer, when we say, "And forgive us our debts as we forgive our debtors." In that moment we forgive one another. God's forgiveness of us and our forgiveness of one another are indissolubly tied together. Both are involved when we say, "I believe in the forgiveness of sins."

In Ephesians 4:32 we Christians are bidden to be kind to one another, tenderhearted, forgiving one another, as God in Christ has forgiven us. The forgiveness of God is the example or model of our forgiveness of each other. In this way, as the following verse says, we can be imitators of God. The forgiveness of God is the *ground* of our forgiveness of one another. It makes it possible. Only because we have been forgiven are we able to forgive. The forgiveness of God *obliges* us to forgive one another. When God has forgiven so much, how can we refuse to forgive? Are we to be like the monstrous servant in Jesus' parable, forgiven by his master of a ten-million-dollar debt, then going out and jailing his fellow servant for a debt of twenty dollars?

In Matthew 6 Jesus says that if we forgive others their trespasses, God also will forgive us; but if we do not forgive others their trespasses, neither will God forgive our trespasses. The door through which the forgiveness of God comes into our lives is the same door through which our forgiveness goes out to others. And if we close the door, letting no forgiveness out, we at the same time prevent any forgiveness from entering in. That's how closely God's forgiveness and our forgiveness are bound together.[23]

Here again, God has given us a sign and a mark: the sacrament of the Lord's Supper. As we take the bread and wine, we act out the reception of God's forgiveness; as we share it, we act out our forgiveness of one another.

When I was at one of our church's seminaries, there was a man in the city who devoted himself to opposing the seminary. He published letters of accusation. He interrupted one of our commencement exercises. He attacked us in the press. One day I found myself sitting very near him at a communion service. I was in a bind. Unless I forgave him it would be hypocritical to commune with him. But if I would not commune with him, I could not commune with the Lord Jesus Christ; I could not receive the forgiveness I needed. It was then I understood for the first time the powerful double connection between the sacrament and the forgiveness of sins.

Let me bring it all to a head. If we want to be able to say the Apostles' Creed with integrity, if we want to savor those transcendent moments in the liturgy where God's forgiveness is declared to us and where we declare that we forgive our debtors, if we want the sacraments of baptism and the Lord's Supper to have their full meaning and power, then before the sun sets we need to find that sister or brother, that soiled fellow saint, who has wronged us, and forgive her, forgive him.

I put my trust, with risk and passion, in the forgiveness of sins.

Lord, we believe; help our unbelief!

25

The Resurrection of the Body and the Life Everlasting

1 Corinthians 15:35–58

"I believe in the resurrection of the body and the life everlasting." The Apostles' Creed ends on a note of triumph, the only triumph that really counts: the triumph over death. For death cancels out all our other triumphs. Death is not only the last enemy but the ever-present enemy that challenges and threatens life at every turn. Just as the second article of the creed reaches its climax in the triumph of Jesus Christ over death, so the third article, and the whole creed, ends with a shout of victory—*our* triumph over death.

But this victory shout is in language that puzzles us, presents real problems for us, is easily misunderstood. We must struggle to explore that language and attempt to clarify it, so that the glorious triumph of believers over death may shine through with fresh power and comfort and challenge.

I

"I believe in the resurrection of the body." Does it bother you to use that language to describe the believer's victory over death? It bothers many people, and for good reason.

For one thing, our common sense tells us that the human body will be dissolved into the elements that make it up. This may happen rather quickly, in cremation, or over a long period of time. But the most massive vaults we can construct will not prevent the final fulfillment of those ancient words of Genesis: "You are dust, and to dust you shall return" (3:19).

So the standard language of the church, for many centuries, has not been "the resurrection of the body" but "the immortality of the soul." Some of us are aware that this language comes from Plato, but it so early entered the church and was so quickly baptized that it is mainline Christian language. It is what we sing about in our hymns—I cannot find a single hymn that speaks clearly of the resurrection of the body. It is what we hear about at funerals, especially in the poetry so often read. It is what we read in the later creeds of the church, including the Westminster Confession of Faith. The picture of it is clear in our minds: the body is the cocoon, the soul is the butterfly. The soul flutters away in the sunlight, and no one has any further regard for the dry, decaying, discarded cocoon. This image is so familiar, so chaste, so free from crass materialism, that we are jarred by the alternate expression: "I believe in the resurrection of the body."

Do we really want the restoration of the old cocoon? Some of us whose connective tissues ache with arthritis, whose nervous systems quake and quiver, whose digestive systems can no longer handle a variety of food (even if we could chew it), whose circulatory systems are clogged with cholesterol, who can neither see well nor hear well, are far from sure that we want this body to rise again. Better to be disembodied than to be chained to what has become a source of weakness, pain, and embarrassment.

A love-hate relationship with our bodies characterizes our culture, whether we are eighty or eighteen. Just watch your television and compute how many of the commercials urge you to love your body: to ease its minor pains and aches, shampoo it, keep it slender, make it smell good, adorn it, beautify it, shave it, fill it with beer, or what have you. We are like Narcissus in the Greek myth who came to a pool in the forest and fell in love with his own reflection. On the same TV, in almost every drama, sooner or later a woman says to a man, "You men are animals. You are only interested in our bodies. You forget we have minds!" And there's the hate side of the love-hate syndrome. Our bodies are the animal part of us. Our minds are the human and humanizing part. So down with the body, up with the mind. Down with the emotions, up with the intellect. Who wants a resurrection of the body? Better to be free of it!

II

In the face of all this, why does the Apostles' Creed speak of the resurrection of the body? For one simple reason: that's the way the Bible speaks. One virtue of an ancient creed is that it carries us back behind Plato to what Karl Barth once called "the strange new world of the Bible."

H. Wheeler Robinson, a great biblical scholar, once put it this way: In biblical thought a human being is "an animated body, not an incarnated soul."[24] Let's chew on that for a minute.

Both biblical thought and our familiar ideas agree that we are more than our bodies. There is something that animates, uses, transcends, completes our bodies. We are some kind of body–spirit or body-soul bond. But in biblical thought, the body part of us is just as much who we are as the spirit part. The body part of us is not bad, to be despised, but good, to be honored. It is not nonessential, to be discarded, but absolutely essential. You are an animated body.

Your body is what identifies you. I wouldn't know how to recognize a disembodied spirit. Would you? Your body is your vehicle of communication. Disembodied spirits may be able to move things around on a Ouija board, though I doubt it. Even if they could, that is pretty colorless communication compared to the rich communication we give out through our bodies—through voice and eye and facial expression and gesture and even posture. The recent books are right when they speak of "body language." Your body is your capacity for relatedness. You are related to the world in all its wonder and beauty and tragedy; you are related to other people; you are even related to God through your body. Your body is your autobiography, though you may never publish one. Oswald McCall puts it unforgettably:

> As year adds to year, that face of yours, which once, like an unwritten page, lay smooth in your baby crib, will take to itself lines, and still more lines, as the parchment of an old historian who jealously sets down all the story. And there, more deep than acids etch the steel, will grow the inscribed narrative of your mental habits, the emotions of your heart, your sense of conscience, your response to duty, what you think of your God and of your fellowmen and of yourself. It will all be there. For men [and women] become like that which they love, and the name thereof is written on their brows.[25]

So when you say you believe in the resurrection of the body, you are not talking at all, I think, about these particular tissues and cells and chromosomes, which have already been replaced in your body several times since you were born, and which will surely decay to dust, whether quickly cremated or preserved at great cost in a vault. You are talking about the pattern, the form, the framework, the shape, which has grown and changed throughout your life yet remains identical to itself, recognizable, a basic and indispensable part of who you are. You are saying you believe in the resurrection of your total self in its unique identity, with its own memory and history, with its intricate, individual web of relationships.

III

Well, you say, that's exactly what I'm talking about when I say "soul"—the total self in its identity and integrity. That may well be true, and I would not want to spend any more time arguing that the Bible's body language is all that different from or superior to the more familiar soul language. It does prevent, I think, wispy, ethereal, vague notions of life after death in which your identity is lost. The Christian hope is not that you will return to God to be lost like a drop of water returns to the ocean and vanishes. You will be you.

The important distinction is not so much between soul and body as between immortality and resurrection. The "immortality of the soul" is often taken to mean that life beyond death is inevitable, it is our right, it is bound to come; death is unreal and powerless in the face of my invincible immortality. I was taught to say in the Child's Catechism, "I have a soul that can never die." The hope of immortality, then, is hope in myself, in who I am and how I am constituted.

"The resurrection of the body" means that death is real and powerful, inevitable, irreversible. The way I am constituted leads to death. As the existentialists say, "Human being is being-unto-death." But the unexpected, the impossible happens: God overturns the sentence of death; God reverses the destruction of death; God raises our essential selves from the dead. The hope of resurrection is not hope in myself but hope in God. That's the important point. That's what we believe with risk and passion!

IV

"But some one will ask," says Paul, " 'How are the dead raised? With what kind of body do they come?' " In answering that question, Paul comes as close as he ever did to telling a parable. It's the familiar parable that Jesus used so many times: the sowing of seed. Paul's point is this: Between the seed corn and the cornstalk there is an identity. The stalk is that seed, but that seed with its limitations removed and its potential realized and therefore very different in appearance, infinitely more useful and glorious. If you had never seen a cornstalk, there is no way you could imagine what one is like by looking at a grain of corn. Just so, we cannot possibly imagine the resurrection body merely by looking at the bodies that we now are. But there will be a connection between the body that you now are and the resurrection body. When God reverses the victory of death—"O death, where is thy victory?"—you will be you: not a drop lost in the illimitable ocean, but you, with a body freed from our space–time limitations, a vehicle unimaginably more appropriate for your identity, your communication, your relationships, your further autobiography, as you are changed from glory to glory in a new kind of life.

V

That brings us to the second phrase describing our triumph over death: "and the life everlasting."

Let me say, simply, that the life promised us beyond death is, in Tillich's phrase, "unambiguous life." The life we now live is ambiguous: full of pain as well as pleasure, sorrow as well as gladness, failure as well as achievement, oppression as well as justice. It is marked by decay and the downhill run. So we feel ambiguous toward it. We have a strong urge to live, and yet we have the death wish. And as we become old and sick, we are profoundly grateful that this ambiguous life does not last forever. But the life of the age to come will be unambiguous, constantly renewed, constantly progressing. Here's where the hymnbook really helps us:

> From sorrow, toil, and pain,
> And sin, we shall be free;
> And perfect love and friendship reign
> Through all eternity.[26]

That is the kind of life we would be willing to have last forever!

I hope, now, that the shout of victory with which the Apostles' Creed ends rings out loud and clear. Because we believe in God the Father Almighty, Maker of heaven and earth, because we believe in Jesus Christ his only Son our Lord, because we believe in the Holy Ghost and in the forgiveness of sins, we can face the future, any future, unafraid. Death's destruction of our essential selves will be reversed, and we shall enter into that unambiguous life, full and abundant, which has no end. Lord, we believe; help our unbelief. Amen.

Part Three

The Ten Commandments

And God spoke all these words, saying,
"I am the LORD your God, who brought you out
of the land of Egypt, out of the house of bondage.
"You will have no other gods before me.
"You will not make for yourself a graven image. . . .
"You will not take the name of the LORD . . . in vain.
"Remember the sabbath day, to keep it holy. . . .
"Honor your father and your mother. . . .
"You will not kill.
"You will not commit adultery.
"You will not steal.
"You will not bear false witness. . . .
"You will not covet. . . ."

Exodus 20:1–17

26

Commandments and Promises

Exodus 19:3–6
Romans 12:1–2

The third part of the Christian primer is the Ten Commandments. When I was a child, copies of the Ten Commandments were on display in public schools as well as in church schools. Every child was expected to know them by heart, and many of us did. They occupied a place of honor in the church's liturgy, especially in the eucharistic liturgy of the Episcopal Church. They occupied a dominant position in the church's catechisms, notably the Shorter and Larger Catechisms used by the Presbyterians. I have a notion they are not nearly so familiar to today's children, yet most have heard of them and have been taught to think of them as a basic part of church teaching.

While Christians speak of ten *commandments,* the Jews speak of ten *words.* That is actually what the original Hebrew of the Bible calls them. All agree that there are *ten* (Ex. 34:28; Deut. 4:13; 10:4), but there are different ways of numbering them. The Jews treat the introductory sentence "I am the LORD . . ." as the first "word." Then they combine the commandment against other gods and the commandment against graven images as a single "word"—the second. Most Christians treat "I am the LORD . . ." as introductory and begin numbering the commandments with the commandment against other gods. Roman Catholics and Lutherans, like the Jews, combine the commandment against other gods with the commandment against graven images, but for them this is the *first* commandment. The commandment against taking the name of the Lord in vain becomes the second commandment, and so on down to the commandment against coveting, which becomes the ninth and tenth commandments: the ninth against coveting your neighbor's house and the tenth against coveting your neighbor's wife, servants, animals, and so on. Most other Christians number the commandments as we shall do in this book.[1]

Again, most agree that the words, or commandments, fall into two groupings, as suggested by the biblical statements that they were written on two tables (Ex. 31:18; 32:15; 34:1, 4, 29; Deut. 9:11, 17; 10:1, 3).[2] But there is disagreement as to whether the groupings are three and seven, four and six, or five and five. The important point is that the first table has to do primarily with duties toward God and the second table with duties toward other human beings. While this is not an absolute distinction, as we shall see, the order is most important. A proper ethic, or system of human interaction, must be preceded by, and rest upon, a proper religion, or relationship between human beings and God. This order reminds us of the Lord's Prayer, where petitions for human needs are preceded by, and rest upon, petitions for God's name, God's kingdom, and God's will. Above all it reminds us of Jesus' famous summary of the commandments: "You shall love the Lord your God with all your heart, and with all your soul, and with all your mind. This is the great and first commandment. And a second is like it, You shall love your neighbor as yourself" (Matt. 22:37–39).

I

In spite of all we have said thus far, there is a real question whether the Ten Commandments belong in a Christian primer. There is a major theological problem involved.

The apostle Paul, you may recall, had some very unkind things to say about "the law." The law *enslaves* (Rom. 7:6,

24; 8:15; Gal. 4:21–31). It promises life, but it *brings death* (Rom. 7:10; 2 Cor. 3:7–11). It arouses our sinful passions (Rom. 7:5, 8). It makes us *know sin* (Rom. 3:20; 7:7). It gives sin its life and strength (Rom. 4:15; 5:13, 20; 7:8–9; 1 Cor. 15:56). By it, sin *kills* us (Rom. 7:11). At bottom, the law is a curse (Gal. 3:10, 13). It is indeed one of the hostile powers over which Christ won his victory on the cross (Gal. 4:3, 8–9; Col. 2:14–15, 20)! What are the Ten Commandments doing in a Christian primer?

Martin Luther shares Paul's negativity toward the law. In the matter of justification, he says, law and gospel must be far asunder. In that context we cannot speak too contemptuously of the law. This does not mean that the law is unprofitable. It has its proper office and use, as indeed everything does. Luther distinguishes two uses. He first mentions the *bridle*. The law bridles the wicked, to the good of the civil commonwealth. Sinful men are curbed (though not inwardly converted) because they fear prison, the sword, and the hangman. Law is, in modern words, a deterrent. The second use that Luther mentions is the *hammer*. By revealing to human beings their sinfulness and God's wrath against sin, it breaks down all self-righteousness and leaves them defenseless. This drives them to seek Christ. "Here it hath an end and it ought to go no further."[3]

John Bunyan is also negative toward the law. You may remember that Christian in *Pilgrim's Progress* loses his way to the Celestial City when he takes the advice of Mr. Worldly Wiseman and turns aside to find Mr. Legality, who dwells in the village of Morality. He passes by Mount Sinai (where the Ten Commandments were given), which almost falls on him and crushes him. He flees from Sinai, where he cannot get rid of his burden, to the cross, where it falls from his back.

All this is in sharp contrast to the Old Testament, where the law is hailed as a joy and a delight. You have only to read Psalm 1 or Psalm 119 to see that for the psalmist the law was the exact opposite of a bridle, a hammer, a curse. It was a blessing, perhaps the greatest of all blessings.

Jesus seems to have shared the psalmist's point of view. Although he demonstrated great freedom toward the law and was accused by the Pharisees of being a lawbreaker, he professed great respect for the law and said he had not come to abolish it but to fulfill it. Whoever does the commandments "and teaches them shall be called great in the kingdom of heaven" (Matt. 5:17–19).

John Calvin is likewise positive toward the law. Although he acknowledges the two uses of the law that Luther set forth, he adds a third that to him is the principal one. The law teaches believers more thoroughly what God's will is and urges them on in well-doing. It belongs in a Christian primer. Those who have been redeemed and want to obey God are shown by the law what that obedience looks like.

In Calvin's Reformed tradition, the Heidelberg Catechism includes the law under the heading of Gratitude. We are grateful to God for delivering and saving us; the law is given us to show us the proper way to say thank you to God. And Karl Barth, standing in the same tradition in our own century, called the law "the other form of the Gospel."

II

Is there any way we can understand or make sense of these sharply contrasting attitudes toward the law within the Christian tradition and within the Bible itself? Let me suggest that we begin by going back to the original setting of the Ten Words. Israel has been enslaved in Egypt. Its very existence has been threatened by deliberate genocide (Exodus 1). God raises up Moses as a deliverer and sends him to Pharaoh with the demand, "Let my people go" (Exodus 2–4). After a protracted struggle with Pharaoh, involving the ten plagues, Israel is commanded to leave Egypt (Exodus 5–12). Pharaoh's army pursues them to the Red Sea, where they are miraculously delivered (Exodus 13–15). God provides for their care and protection in the wilderness and brings them to Sinai (Exodus

16–18). There before the mountain, God speaks to them as follows:

> You have seen what I did to the Egyptians, and how I bore you on eagles' wings and brought you to myself. Now therefore, if you will obey my voice and keep my covenant, you shall be my own possession among all peoples; for all the earth is mine, and you shall be to me a kingdom of priests and a holy nation.
>
> *Exodus 19:4–6*

The Ten Words, which follow in Exodus 20, are not a recipe for gaining God's favor; Israel already has God's favor. They are not requirements for being delivered from bondage; Israel has already been delivered from bondage. They are a description of what it will be like to live as God's own people. They are the rubrics for Israel's function as a kingdom of priests before God in behalf of the Gentiles.[4] They spell out the lifestyle of a holy nation.

Now we see the significance of the fact noted earlier that for the Jews the first word is: "I am the LORD your God, who brought you out of the land of Egypt, out of the house of bondage." Grace precedes duty. That word must never be omitted, no matter how we number it. In Jan Lochman's brilliant figure, it is the sign that precedes the brackets, changing everything within the brackets.[5] Seen in this context, it is no wonder that the Ten Words were not seen by Israel as a fresh enslavement, a death-dealing curse. "Israel certainly did not understand the Decalogue as an absolute moral law prescribing ethics: she rather recognized it as a revelation vouchsafed to her at a particular moment in her history, through which she was offered the saving gift of life."[6]

How, then, are we to understand the negative attitude toward the law in the writings of Paul? There was abroad in his time, particularly among the Pharisee party, of which he was a member, a misunderstanding of the law. Obedience to the law was understood as the way to deliverance; if all Israel would keep the law perfectly from one Sabbath to the next, the Messiah would come and deliver them from the Roman yoke. "Works of the law" were the way to personal righteousness. Zealous Jewish Christians were seeking to impose all the details of Jewish law on Paul's Gentile converts. Paul is warning those converts that to accept this understanding of the law would be a fresh enslavement, leading to death, not life. It is easy to understand how Luther, fighting the ideas of "merit" and "good works" that were abroad in medieval Catholicism, would find Paul's negativity so congenial.

We need to remember those other words of Paul that tend to agree with the attitude of the psalmists and of Jesus. "The law is holy, and the commandment is holy and just and good" (Rom. 7:12). "I of myself serve the law of God with my mind" (Rom. 7:25). "Love is the fulfilling of the law" (Rom. 13:10). "Do we then overthrow the law by this faith? By no means! On the contrary, we uphold the law" (Rom. 3:31). And Luther, for all his harsh words about the law, includes the Ten Commandments in his catechism.

III

The positive, life-giving aspect of the Ten Words is variously described by recent writers. Andrew Greeley says this is a liturgical, not a legal, text.[7] Jan Lochman asks whether emphasis on the Ten Commandments denies a theology of grace and answers yes, if they are regarded as timeless, universal laws, interpreted legalistically; no, if they are tied to the great liberation recounted in Exodus. When the revelation of the commands is seen as a saving, liberating event, they become the Magna Carta of the covenant, a charter of freedom. We should speak of the Ten Freedoms.[8] Walter Harrelson says the Ten Words are "more akin to statements about the character of life in community than they are to cases of violation of law . . . and what punishment is to be dealt out." They are more like a bill of rights than a criminal code.[9] Walter Brueggemann speaks of "the envisioning of an alternative humanity which is implicit in the claims of the commandments." The commandments, he says, are "the route of present people into the promised community."[10] Bruce Larson speaks of the Ten Commandments as God's dream for us and says, "The law is meant to help us fulfill that dream."[11]

I propose that we think together about the Ten Words as the "Ten Promises." I have become convinced in a lifetime of trying to expound the Bible that there is a promise implicit in every demand God lays on us, just as there is a demand implicit in every promise God makes to us. Both are there in the Ten Words. But, since for centuries we have emphasized the demand side of those Words, let us try, for a change, to emphasize the promise side.

An emphasis on the promise side will avoid the false legalism against which Paul and Luther inveigh. The grace of God will not be obscured but will be brought to the fore. An emphasis on the promise side will inevitably stress the corporate nature of the Ten Words. They picture what the corporate life of God's people will be like when God's dreams for them come true. An emphasis on the promise side will turn our attention to the future. Grammatically, most of the Ten Words are in the future tense. Some scholars believe that originally all of them were.[12] Although Hebrew has an imperative, the usual way to express a prohibition was not with a negative imperative but with a negative future. So our usual translation—"thou shalt not"—is entirely legitimate. But a negative future can also express a promise: "As my people you will not have other gods, you will not make graven images to worship . . . you will not kill, commit adultery, steal, lie, covet." Imagine a society where those things, so characteristic of the world as we know it, simply no longer happen. What a promise!

The demand remains, transformed. Instead of hedging life about with a list of no-no's, the Ten Words demand this of us: "Having received the promises, live as though the future were now, as though the kingdom has already come, as though you really are God's peculiar people, God's own possession." Not as simple as ticking off prohibitions? True enough. But much more fun, and closer to the ultimate truth. I think it is the same truth Paul had in mind when he appealed to the Romans by the mercies of God: "Do not be conformed to this world but be transformed by the renewal of your mind, that you may prove what is the will of God, what is good and acceptable and perfect" (Rom. 12:2).

Welcome to an exploration of the Ten Promises.

27

The First Promise:
Getting It Together

Isaiah 44:6–8
Luke 14:25–33

You will have no other gods before me.
                              Exodus 20:3

"I promise you, my covenant people, that the time will come when all your other gods will disappear, when I alone will be your God." Hasn't that time already come for us? Aren't we Christians all monotheists, believers in only one God? Haven't we rejected polytheism, the belief in many gods, as heathen superstition? Don't we assent to those sonorous words from Isaiah: "I am the first and I am the last; besides me there is no god. . . . Is there a God besides me? There is no Rock; I know not any" (Isa. 44:6, 8)? Well, as my mother used to say, we shall see.

I

What is a god? Paul Tillich offers this definition: "Gods are beings who transcend the realm of ordinary experience in power and meaning, with whom human beings have relations which surpass ordinary relations in intensity and significance."[13] That gets at the extraordinary nature of gods. But we need to go on and talk about those extraordinary relations that human beings have with them. Martin Luther said long ago, "Whatever then thy

heart clings to and relies upon, that is properly thy God."
The British theologian H. H. Farmer speaks in terms of
unconditional demand and final succor. Whatever we recognize as placing a demand on our lives that is ultimate
and as offering help, comfort, succor beyond which there
is no other help—that is our God.[14] The American theologian H. Richard Niebuhr works with the ideas of value and
loyalty. Whatever gives me value, affirms my being, is the
center of my confidence and trust; whatever at the same
time engenders my loyalty, my fidelity—that is my God.[15]
It is not difficult to discern substantial agreement between
Luther, Farmer, and Niebuhr. On one hand we cling to
God, we are loyal to God, we acknowledge God's unconditional demand upon us. On the other hand we rely on
God, God is the center of our confidence, God is our final
succor.

II

Now then, as we look at our world, our society, our
church, ourselves, do we see people with a single supreme
loyalty or people divided and torn between many compet-
ing loyalties? Do we see people who rely on one final,
ultimate source of help and security or people whose trust
is divided among many different centers of confidence?
Do we see people with one God or with many gods?

One of the things that happens to us in our youth is that
we develop a great capacity for loyalty, fierce loyalty. Boy
Scout Troop Ten was not a very good troop. In fact, lots
of the time we didn't even have a scoutmaster, and almost
nobody ever went on to the Eagle rank. But I recall being
so fiercely loyal to Troop Ten that if anybody suggested
there was a better troop anywhere in the world he would
certainly have had a fight on his hands. Loyalties among
teens to gangs, schools, colleges, fraternities, sororities,
military outfits, athletic teams, and so on are well known.

Young people are not only finding within themselves
this capacity for fierce and unquestioning loyalty—good or
bad—they are also searching for a center of confidence.

You see, they've just discovered that the people they had confidence in when they were children—the adults—are stupid. If you don't believe that, ask the teenagers and they'll tell you. So they're looking for someone else to trust. And one reason, I think, for torrid teen love affairs is that they're saying, "I've found you, and maybe you are the one in whom I can put my confidence, put my life and all that I am and have in your hands."

Now what rips this beautiful picture of loyalty and confidence that we develop in our youth is that there is no one supreme center of confidence or one supreme locus of loyalty. Life becomes unraveled: you put your trust in this one day, and the next day you decide you really can't trust it after all, so you try something else. You're feverishly loyal over here one day, but the next day you've shifted your loyalty over there. Life becomes ragged and unsatisfactory and complex and multiple instead of singular. I can remember back to my days as a young person being just like a rope in a tug-of-war—pulled this way and then pulled that way.

This does not automatically correct itself with age. Our coins say "In God We Trust." But who will stand on the floor of Congress and advocate that we transfer to the living God the trust we place in nuclear deterrence? Who will advocate that we transfer to the God of all nations the loyalty that we give to national security? Such ideas as national security and nuclear deterrence certainly "transcend the realm of ordinary experience in power and meaning." Any suggestion that they are subject to debate or question is regarded as blasphemy. And blasphemy is irreverent speech about a god.

The past may be easier for us to handle than the present. I recall vividly a debate in a southern church body in the 1950s where one speaker said, "Don't try to prove to me from the Bible that segregation is wrong. If you succeed, you will have taken my Bible away from me!" It was clear that for him the institution of segregation did "transcend the realm of ordinary experience in power and meaning." It was a clear rival of the God of the Bible, in whom he wanted to believe if he could. It was also clear which would win if it came to a contest.

How many adults are torn between the demands of the boss and the demands of their consciences? International law, since the Nuremberg trials, clearly says that the demands of superiors in the army or the state are not unconditional. But how many are willing to take the risk of disobedience? How many, on the other hand, are ready to applaud as a hero one who flaunts law and morality in order to carry out the superior's wishes? Where are those who will say, "We must obey God's orders rather than human orders" (Acts 5:29, adapted)?

We are besieged hourly by advertisements urging us to find our ultimate succor in *things,* from headache powders to palatial homes. We are to achieve status with others and meaning for ourselves, not from God but from conspicuous consumption. When you own a certain automobile, we are told, "you have everything." There could hardly be a clearer statement of a rival god.

Alas, we are monotheists in theory but polytheists in practice. And this is at the root of our restlessness, our inner dividedness, our lack of integrity. This is why we can't get it all together, to use that wonderful phrase from the youth culture. The letter of James describes us: double-minded people, unstable in all our ways (James 1:8). Only by faith in the One can our lives be unified.

III

Now the First Promise, and it is a great one, is the promise of conversion, the discovery that there is one living and true God and that everything falls into place when we put our supreme trust and supreme loyalty in that God alone. All the lesser trusts and loyalties shake out and find their proper place. We get it all together. We become one person instead of a quarreling committee. All the votes come together into a silent, powerful sense of the meeting. It does not often happen instantly or perfectly or unfailingly, but monotheism becomes the hope and goal and direction of our lives.

God offers that to us as members of the Christian community. Together we can be a people who have one supreme center of confidence and one supreme center of loyalty, one God! Together we can declare, "We confess and acknowledge one God alone, to whom alone we must cleave, whom alone we must serve, whom only we must worship, and in whom alone we put our trust."[16] Corporately we can remind ourselves, "We acknowledge no other God. We must not set our ultimate reliance on any other help. We must not yield unconditional obedience to any other power. We must not love anyone or anything more than we love God."[17]

The First Promise is basic to the other nine. We will never be a people free from killing and adultery and theft and lying and covetousness and all the rest until we have a single center of loyalty and confidence. We do those things because we are still divided within ourselves, still switching from one god to another.

Years ago, in a small group, the young wife of a seminary professor made a remark that I've never forgotten. She had been raised pagan; she was a new Christian. And she said to us, "For a long time now I have thought that I could not live if anything happened to my husband. But I have come to see that, as hard as it would be, I could live without him. The one I cannot live without is God." She had received the First Promise. She had been seeking the solution to her loneliness and all her other needs in another human being. But now she knew what the priorities were, and life had fallen into place. "The one I cannot live without is God."

IV

This simple story may help us in understanding that extraordinarily difficult passage from Luke's Gospel which is our suggested New Testament reading. Jesus clearly intended to shock his listeners when he said, "You've got to hate your father and mother, wife, children, brothers, sisters, and even your own life." Jesus is the one who said that the second great commandment is to love your neighbor as yourself; and these are our closest neighbors. And Jesus said also that hatred is a poison that destroys the hater and puts us in danger of the hell of fire. So Jesus cannot have meant these words literally—to hate. What he is saying, I think, is that these persons and things cannot be your gods. They cannot be your ultimate center of confidence or your ultimate center of loyalty. Neither can your own life. There is a healthy self-confidence and self-preservation, but when self becomes the ultimate center of confidence and the ultimate center of loyalty, selfishness is there like a poison. Self-preservation is not the first law of life The first law of life is what the Shorter Catechism says it is: "To glorify God, and to enjoy [God] forever."

Then Jesus said (with that final remark about giving up all that you have) that your possessions cannot be the center of your confidence and the center of your loyalty. What twisted lives we lead when that happens to us, as our TV culture insists it must! But you really can't take it with you.

Dream with me. What would it be like if we really had no other gods? How many split and divided people would be healthy and whole again? How many burned-out people would be full of zeal and energy once more? How many of our conflicts would seem ridiculous? How many of our problems would be resolved? What unity we would experience as we come together to worship one God alone! Even our disinterested young people might sense that we are really getting it together and find models and guidance for the complex problems that face them.

"You will have no other gods before me." A commandment, yes, but what a promise! What a promise!

28

The Second Promise:
No Idols

Exodus 32
1 Corinthians 8

You will not make for yourself a graven image, or any likeness of anything that is in heaven above, or that is in the earth beneath, or that is in the water under the earth; you will not bow down to them or serve them; for I the LORD your God am a jealous God, visiting the iniquity of the fathers upon the children to the third and the fourth generation of those who hate me, but showing steadfast love to thousands of those who love me and keep my commandments.

Exodus 20:4-6

We continue on our way through the Ten Commandments—or, as we have begun to call them, the Ten Promises—ten pictures of life ordered and lived in a more meaningful and liberated and compassionate and beautiful way than we generally live.

The picture of life in the First Promise was, you remember, of life free from an inner tug-of-war, the sort of Jekyll and Hyde existence where we are pulled in many different directions because we have many gods and many centers of trust and loyalty. We are promised a life free from that, a life ordered and simple and unified because we have only one God. We will worship that one God, and all the other centers of trust and loyalty will fall in line behind that supreme, ultimate center.

The picture of life in the Second Commandment or the Second Promise is a life free from idols—free from the false worship of gods we can make for ourselves and therefore control and manipulate. These two promises obviously overlap. It is not always easy to keep them separate or to distinguish one from the other. Indeed, the last part of the Second Promise seems to belong more properly with the First! We can understand why, as we noted in chapter 26, the Jews, the Roman Catholics, and the Lutherans lump these two together as a single commandment. However that may be, the problem of rival gods is important enough to warrant a second discussion.

I

One way of getting at the meaning of the Second Promise is to retell the fascinating stories in Exodus that paint such a vivid contrast between false worship and true worship. Moses went up on the mountain, so the story goes, and stayed there for forty days and forty nights while the Lord gave him, in great detail, the design for the tabernacle, for the movable tent in which true worship should be carried out. Meanwhile, down at the foot of the mountain, the people were growing restless waiting for Moses. So they decided to appoint liturgical teams and to plan and devise their own worship. They gathered around Aaron the priest, and they said, "Up, make us gods, who shall go before us; as for this Moses, the man who brought us up out of the land of Egypt, we do not know what has become of him." We're tired, they were saying, of an unseen, invisible God whose presence is perhaps symbolized to us by a pillar of fire at night and a pillar of cloud by day, which is sometimes there and sometimes not and which we can't control. We want a god we can get our hands on—a god who will always be there when we need him—a god we have made ourselves.

Aaron made no protest. He may have felt the same way.

But at any rate he asked for all their gold rings. So in they came—a great pile of nose rings and earrings and finger rings. And he took the whole pile and melted it down and molded it, and he got out his engraving tools and engraved it. And there was a beautiful, shining, golden calf! The people were happy because finally they had a god like all their neighbors had. It's hard, you know, being the only one on the block without a visible god. "There are your gods, O Israel, who brought you up out of the land of Egypt!" cried Aaron. He made an altar in front of the calf and proclaimed that the next day would be a great feast day unto Yahweh, the Lord. We're not departing from the Lord, he said. We're just getting him where we can see him and get our hands on him and control him.

So the next day they sacrificed animals and offered burnt offerings to the calf and had a big feast. They did all of the things to the calf that they had learned to do to the invisible Presence of the Lord. Right in the middle of things, just as they had rolled the rugs back and were beginning to have a big dance, who came down from the mountain but Moses!

Moses got so mad, when he saw what was going on, he broke the tablets of the law that he had under his arms. He took the calf; he burned it; he ground it into powder; he scattered it on the camp water supply and made the people drink the water. This somewhat cowed Aaron; in fact, it scared him nearly to death. So he came up with a story. He said, Moses, I didn't make that calf. I just threw the gold in the fire and the calf came out. Nice try, Aaron, but that really makes no difference. The point is not just how the calf was molded and engraved. The point is that the calf cannot judge the sins of Israel, and the calf cannot forgive the sins of Israel, and the calf cannot lead Israel. The calf cannot even move.

John Calvin wrote long ago, "Human beings are so stupid that they fasten God whenever they fashion God."[18] That's idolatry.

After Moses had cooled off a little, he went ahead with plans for the tabernacle, the plans he had received up on the mountain. Beautiful hangings on posts made a large enclosure open to the sky. As we enter that enclosure we see the great altar for the burnt offerings and the big laver where the priests wash up after all they do for the offerings. Toward the other end of the enclosure is a roofed tent, the tabernacle itself. In the front room, the Holy Place, we see the altar of incense and the golden candlestick and the table for the bread of the Presence. Behind those things is a curtain. Behind that curtain is the Holy of Holies. And if we were permitted to enter there, we would see the Ark of the Covenant, a chest of wood covered with gold inside and out. The lid of the Ark serves as a portable throne, a seat for Yahweh. There are some carved figures there, the cherubim with their wings. They do not represent the divine Presence; they protect the divine Presence from our curious gaze. On that throne, protected by those wings, in the seat of power and authority—nothing! No image. No representation of anything in heaven above or in the earth beneath or in the waters under the earth. There in that holiest of all holy places is nothing that human beings could mold or engrave, just the invisible Presence of a God who is so mighty and so incomprehensible that there is no way we can represent that God at all.

II

"Well," you say, "I understand all that. But it doesn't concern me. I may have broken a lot of the commandments, but I have never made a graven image. There may be people in some remote corners of the globe who do that kind of thing, but I've never seen anybody do it, and I have never done it myself, and I have no plans or desire to do it."

That's right. I'm not worried about your behaving like that man who was held up to such ridicule in Isaiah 44. He cuts down a tree, burns part of it in the heating stove to warm his house, burns another part of it in the cooking stove to roast his meat, and then he says, "What can I do with the rest of it?" And after he is warmed and fed, he says. "I'll make a god out of it." So he carves it into an idol, falls down and worships it, prays to it, and says, "Deliver me, for you are my god." You are not going to do that.

Like the Corinthians in our New Testament reading, you know that "an idol has no real existence" (1 Cor. 8:4). Yet there was a constant danger of idolatry in the church at Corinth (1 Cor. 5:11). In the sixteenth century, John Calvin remarked that "scarcely a single person has ever been found who did not fashion for himself an idol or specter in place of God."[19] As Andrew Greeley pungently remarks, "The last of the golden calves was not the one Moses destroyed."[20] You are not going to make an old Model-T idol, but you may make a modern one with front-wheel drive and computerized fuel injection.

Paul Tillich says that idolatry is nothing else than bestowing ultimate concern on what is not truly ultimate.[21] Let's unpack that statement. We're concerned about a lot of things: what we shall eat and what we shall drink and how we shall be clothed. We're concerned about our children and their education. We're concerned about hospital insurance and the latest surgery. We're concerned about the disturbing things we read about in the newspaper or see on TV. We're concerned about many things, and they are important. But the only thing worthy of our ultimate concern is that which makes the difference between being and non-being—that which makes the difference between whether there is a world (and you and me and human society and culture and all that makes life meaningful and purposeful and valuable) or whether there is nothing at all. When we give ultimate concern to things or objects or even people who cannot create or guarantee the meaning and purpose and value of life as a whole, we make that thing or object or person an idol.

For example, you have some graven images in your pocket or pocketbook: a graven image of George Washington, with an eagle on the reverse side; a graven image of Franklin D. Roosevelt, with a torch on the reverse side; a graven image of Thomas Jefferson, with Monticello on the reverse side; a graven image of Abraham Lincoln, with the Lincoln Memorial on the reverse side. There they are. These images cannot give meaning and purpose and value to life. They cannot convict you of sin or forgive your sin. They cannot bring you to judgment or grant you mercy. They offer you no hope beyond death. Having eyes, they cannot see; having ears, they cannot hear; having mouths, they cannot speak. They cannot carry you anywhere. You have to carry them. Yet many people bestow on these graven images their ultimate concern.

Let me tell you two stories. I cannot remember where I read either one of them. The first story is about a woman who was admitted to a mental hospital. She had her right fist clenched. She wouldn't open that fist to shake hands, to wash herself or put on her clothes, to feed herself, to open a door. Finally the attendants seized her and forced her fist open. She screamed as though she were being murdered. In her fist were two or three coins. It was clear that her sense of identity, worth, and security was all tied up with those two or three coins. This is exaggerated, bizarre behavior, but is it a parable of your life and mine?

The other story is about a man fleeing from a burning city in time of war, going down to the water's edge, finding a small boat, and getting on board clutching to his chest a wooden chest full of heavy oriental coins. As the boat got out to the middle of the river, water began to come over the gunwales. People said, "We've got to lighten the weight in the boat. Everybody throw overboard whatever they brought with them." The man refused to part with his chest of coins. Finally, they took it from him by force and tossed it overboard. Immediately he plunged after it, and since he could not swim, he drowned. That chest had become more important to him than life itself. Is that a parable of your life and mine?

It is a strange thing about these graven images of ours. On every one of them, in small letters, you can read, "In God We Trust." It's as though somebody wanted to say to us as we handle these images, Please don't give this coin your ultimate concern. Put your trust in God. It's as

though far back in our history somewhere somebody saw
the direction in which we were moving and tried to de-
contaminate these graven images and keep them from
becoming idols. How many of us ever see or think about
those words on our coins?

Of course money is not the only idol. We can make
nation or race our ultimate concern. We can be concerned
ultimately about family heritage or social position, about
a creed or a hymnbook, about an economic system or a
political system, about a church building or church government. We can be ultimately concerned about any
number of things, creatures of our own hands, that we can
bow down to and serve, provoking God to jealousy.

We need to pause for a moment on the words "I the
Lord your God am a jealous God." Is God saying that the
Lord of the universe is moved to jealousy by the idolatry
of someone as insignificant as you are? Yes, God feels pain
when you fail to love God with all your heart and all your
mind and all your soul and all your strength, and when you
foolishly bestow that love on idols, to your own hurt and
shame. And in our inadequate human language the best
word to describe that pain is "jealousy." God, says Andrew
Greeley, is here revealed as an aroused, passionate lover.[22]
What an amazing bit of gospel in the midst of law!

It is sadly true that children raised in a home where
idolatry is practiced will have great difficulty in adopting
for themselves a true standard of values and will be apt to
pass false values on to their children. We need not deny
that the just hand of God is in that process. But God's
delight is to show steadfast love to thousands who love God
and keep God's commandments.

III

Now this is not only the Second Commandment—"You
must not worship idols." It is the Second Promise—"If you
will be my covenant people, I promise you that you will
have a common life together in which you will not be
burdened by idols." Hallelujah! What would that be like?

Can you even imagine a society or a church in which money is no longer an idol, no longer a center of ultimate concern, where people are free to think of other things than how to make a fast buck, where human power and human position and human fame are not as important as God and the will of God and the kingdom of God? Wouldn't such a life be more meaningful and liberated, more compassionate and beautiful, than the way we generally live?

Our idols are burdens. In Isaiah 46 the prophet makes fun of the Babylonians who were fleeing from the approaching Persian army, carrying their idols with them. What a ridiculous sight the idols are, bobbing up and down on the backs of cattle! What a contrast there is between idols and the living God! You made them, but God made you. You carry them, but God carries you. The living God is not a burden, but a boost; not a load, but a lift. It would be an incredible relief to be unburdened of our idols.

It has been my privilege to visit several experiments in Christian community where there has been a deliberate attempt to live without idols. Most of the people have practiced downward mobility in order to join the community. They live purposely below the poverty level. They do not seek fame or advertise themselves. They do not seek power. They devote themselves to serving the poor, among whom, if we believe Matthew 25, Jesus is hidden. Their common life is not free from problems, for community living is not easy. But even a visitor can sense the simplicity and joy and—yes—the power of a different kind that permeates the community.

I always come away from those visits haunted by a dream. What if a local church—my local church—could be idol free? What if my town, my country, the world could be like that? That is God's promise to us: "You will not make for yourselves idols. . . . You will not bow down to them and serve them." The question is: Do we dare to live by that promise, not just in a few obscure experiments but out in the world that will take us for fools?

29

The Third Promise: No Empty Name

Ezekiel 39:7–8, 25–29
Philippians 2:1–11

You will not take the name of the LORD your God in vain,
for the LORD will not hold that one guiltless who takes
[God's] name in vain.

Exodus 20:7

This is commonly understood as a commandment
against cursing, swearing, profanity. Certainly that is involved, and certainly that is important. I remember from
my navy days a grizzled bo'sun's mate who could swear for
three minutes without drawing a breath and without re-
peating himself once. While few of us may be that expert,
is any one of us altogether innocent? As it is written in the
book of James (3:2), if anyone makes no mistakes with the
tongue, that one is a perfect person, able to bridle the
whole body also. The Third Commandment may be the
most widely violated of all the commandments, except
perhaps for the Tenth: You will not covet.

I

Profanity is a weak, despicable, irreverent habit. But I
do not believe it is the most serious violation of the Third
Commandment. Recent Old Testament scholarship says
that what is forbidden here is not so much the empty, vain

use of God's name as its use to do harm. One suggested translation is, "You shall not lift up the name of Yahweh for mischief."[23] Calvin saw this long ago. There is much evil, he says, in the empty and wicked abuse of God's name whereby it is rendered contemptible. But "it is a much greater sin if it be put to abominable uses, as those do who make it serve the superstitions of necromancy, frightful curses, unlawful exorcisms, and other wicked incantations."[24] This sounds rather medieval, but it is clear that Calvin is condemning the use of God's name, which is powerful to bless and heal, to do harm instead.

Names are enormously important in the Bible. The names of people are not just handles so we can differentiate John Q. Smith from John P. Smith. A person's name expresses that person's character, sums up that person's worth and essence. So if a person's character, worth, and essence change, the name must be changed. Abram becomes Abraham, Sarai becomes Sarah, Jacob becomes Israel, Simon becomes Peter, Saul becomes Paul.

The name of God, then, is an expression of God's character, worth, and essence. It carries with it some of God's power.[25] In stories like the wrestling of Jacob (Genesis 32) and Moses at the burning bush (Exodus 3), God is reticent to reveal the divine name. This is understandable when we realize that to know the name of something or someone is to have power over that thing or person. A vivid expression of this is the familiar fairy story of the maiden who was enslaved by an evil fairy until she learned his name was Rumpelstiltskin. Knowing his name broke his power over her and gave her power over him. So when God graciously reveals the divine name to us, we are given power over God. It is an act of great risk. When we misuse that power for our own selfish purposes or to do harm to others, we are disobeying the Third Commandment in a far more serious way than just slipping out a blasphemous curse word.

When a politician uses the name of God to get votes, when a televangelist uses the name of God to line his pockets with millions, the Third Commandment is violated. When we say that God-fearing Americans have the right and duty to rain down nuclear destruction on the godless Russians or to wage surrogate guerrilla warfare on the godless Nicaraguans, we have taken up the name of God for mischief. We may have legitimate political quarrels with the governments of Russia and Nicaragua, but there are millions of devout, practicing Christians in the Soviet Union, as well as many Jews. And Nicaragua is one of the most deeply religious nations on earth. Let us not use the name of God to justify their destruction.

II

The Larger Catechism carries us even deeper into the seriousness of this commandment. It asks (Q. 113): "What are the sins forbidden in the Third Commandment?" And after listing profanity and superstition and perjury and "vain janglings" and the like, it goes on to include being ashamed of the name of God.

We suggested as our New Testament reading a remarkable passage from Philippians 2. It declares that as a result of Jesus' obedience unto death, even death on a cross, God has highly exalted him and given him the name that is above every name. That is to say that the character and worth and essence and name of God have been bestowed on Jesus Christ.

Now then, have you ever been ashamed of that name, been in a crowd where you wanted to conceal the fact that you are a Christian? Like Peter, have you denied with an oath that you ever knew him? How well I remember from my teen years occasions when we sat around and tried to see who could be or pretend to be toughest, most worldly, most wicked—not at all Christian, for pity's sake! It was part of the macho thing. Do you know even now the secret shame of being a Christian? That is far more serious than profanity or "vain janglings."

III

The catechism goes on: being ashamed *of* the name of God or a shame *to* the name of God. "We bear the name of Christians, his name and sign we bear"—so runs the familiar hymn. And have we so acted and lived as to bring shame to that name? Oh, the memory of those incidents is a bitter memory in my own life. The tragedy is that we are all caught up in a system, a way of life, that constantly brings shame to the name of God, especially as that name has been bestowed upon Christ.

One of my favorite saints is John Woolman, the Quaker tailor who lived in the American colonies before the American Revolution. Toward the end of his life he had a dream, which I will let him recount in his own words:

> In a time of sickness, a little more than two years and a half ago, I was brought so near the gates of death that I forgot my name. . . . I was then carried in the spirit to the mines where poor oppressed people were digging rich treasures for those called Christians, and heard them blaspheme the name of Christ, at which I was grieved, for his name to me was precious. I was then informed that these heathens were told that those who oppressed them were the followers of Christ, and they said among themselves, "If Christ directed them to use us in this sort, then Christ is a cruel tyrant."[26]

There is to me no more solemn word in scripture than Romans 2:24: "As it is written, the name of God is blasphemed among the Gentiles because of you." It is extraordinarily difficult to make Christian converts among Native Americans. Why? Because Christians came across the great waters, took away their sacred tribal lands, forced them to walk the Trail of Tears, introduced them to smallpox, venereal diseases, and alcoholism, broke treaties, declared that the only good Indian is a dead Indian. "The name of God is blasphemed among the Gentiles because of you." How can we talk to our Jewish neighbors about Jesus Christ in the face of the long record of the persecution of Jews by Christians, culminating in the holocaust in

Christian Germany? That Jesus Christ bears God's name is not accepted by Jews because of you.

The suggested reading from Ezekiel tells us that God is jealous for God's name. God does not take it lightly when we bring shame on the divine name. The Lord will not hold that one guiltless who takes the Lord's name in vain.

IV

The Ten Commandments, we have said, are also Ten Promises. And if the sins here are great ones, the promises are equally great.

"I promise," says the Lord, "that among my covenant people there will be no more careless, empty swearing, cursing, and profanity. No, there will be great silences. And when the name of God is spoken out of silence it will be heavy, weighty, full of awe, and full of blessing." I like to think that as the name of God receives its true weight once again, all our other words will be weightier. The world is full of talk that doesn't mean anything; it's only talk, empty sound filling up empty minutes and hours, light as a feather. But if out of reverence for the name of God there is less talk and more silence among us, maybe even our ordinary language will regain weight and meaning and worth.

"I promise," says the Lord, "that among my covenant people my name will not be used for mischief, to justify war and hatred. The power over me that I have given my people in giving them my name will not be used for selfish purposes, but for the advancement of my rule on earth as it is in heaven.

"I promise," says the Lord, "that my people will not be ashamed of my name." "Take the name of Jesus with you," says the gospel hymn, "take it wheresoe'er you go." No more secret shame of being a Christian.

"I promise," says the Lord, "that you will not bring shame on my name and cause it to be blasphemed among

the Gentiles. No, they will see your good works and give
glory to your Father who is in heaven.

"And I promise," says the Lord, "that you will not call
on my name in vain. Promises of answered prayer are tied
to your knowledge of my name. Whatever you ask for in
my name will be done for you!" (John 14:13–14; 15:16;
16:23–24).

> I know a soul that is steeped in sin,
>   That no man's art can cure;
> But I know a Name, a Name, a Name
>   That can make that soul all pure.
>
> I know a life that is lost to God,
>   Bound down by the things of earth;
> But I know a Name, a Name, a Name
>   That can bring that soul new birth.
>
> I know of lands that are sunk in shame,
>   Of hearts that faint and tire;
> But I know a Name, a Name, a Name
>   That can set those lands on fire.[27]

You shall not take that Name in vain. A solemn commandment. You will not take that Name in vain. A glorious
promise!

V

Are there any connections between the Third Promise
and the dominant fact of our age, the possibility of nuclear
holocaust? I'm not sure there are connections, but my
mind keeps making them because both things are so much
on my mind.

Here's one. Suppose an all-out nuclear exchange occurs
and the clouds of radioactive dust drift eastward and
southward to poison air and water and the food chain in
the predominantly non-Christian lands of our planet, and
they ask, "Who brought this upon us?" If the answer is
"The nations of the Christian West," and the Gentiles

begin to blaspheme the name of Christ, that would be the ultimate violation of the Third Commandment.

Here's another. If an all-out nuclear exchange occurs and people begin to call in anguish and in earnest on the name of the Lord, they will not call in vain. I do not mean that God will reach out a great hand and catch the bombs before they hit. I do not mean that those who are burned will not die, that those who are irradiated will not suffer. I do not even mean that some remnants of the human race will surely be preserved. We may all go, as many scientists now believe. What I mean is that a nuclear holocaust will not be the end of God. It will not erase God's signature from the universe or God's name from our hearts. God is more than equal to the worst we can do. God proved that once in the resurrection of Jesus. God can prove it again in the re-creation of a planet—new heavens and a new earth in which righteousness dwells. And that would be the ultimate fulfilment of the Third Promise.

We know a Name, a Name, a Name.

30

The Fourth Promise: Rest

Jeremiah 17:19–27
Mark 2:23–28

Remember the sabbath day, to keep it holy. Six days you will labor, and do all your work; but the seventh day is a sabbath to the LORD your God; in it you will not do any work, you, or your son, or your daughter, your manservant, or your maidservant, or your cattle, or the sojourner who is within your gates; for in six days the LORD made heaven and earth, the sea, and all that is in them, and rested the seventh day; therefore the LORD blessed the sabbath day and hallowed it.

Exodus 20:8–11

Observe the sabbath day, . . . that your manservant and your maidservant may rest as well as you. You will remember that you were a servant in the land of Egypt, and the LORD your God brought you out thence with a mighty hand and an outstretched arm; therefore the LORD your God commanded you to keep the sabbath day.

Deuteronomy 5:12, 14–15

In a private Christian school the religion instructor decided to experiment with periods of silence in his classes. The teacher was wise and slowly increased the time until his students learned to be comfortable for ten minutes, not doing or saying anything, just *being*. The students were grateful. One said, "It is the only time in my day when I am not expected to achieve something." But some parents were very upset. One said, "It just isn't Christian!" Another said, "I'm not paying all that tuition for my child to sit there and do nothing."

In that little story, told by Tilden Edwards,[28] the problems of the Fourth Commandment come into focus. The Fourth Commandment calls us to observe a day, one in seven, when we don't work. Is it really legitimate not to work in a world where there is so much to be done and we're so far behind? Is such a time of nonworking helpful in making us more fit for the time when we go back to work? Is such a time of value in and for itself? The Fourth Commandment says yes to all three of those questions. And that makes it a commandment that is full of promise, full of good news for us all.

I

I can remember that as a boy I did not find the Fourth Commandment very promising. I was dreadfully bored. I was bored at Sunday school and I was bored in church, especially during "the long prayer" that went on and on. I was bored in the time between getting home from church and eating dinner. I could not read the Sunday comics—the funny paper, we called it. That was put away until Monday. I could not listen to the radio, unless it was church music or a church service, and I'd had enough of that. I could not pick a fight with my brother. I could not play a competitive sport. A concession was made to a small boy in need of physical activity. I could go out and toss a tennis ball up on the roof and let it roll back to me. Just why that was lawful on the Sabbath I didn't fully understand, but I was grateful. I suspect the gutters of that dear house are still clogged with tennis balls that never came back.

After dinner my father and mother lay down for naps. At my present age, I understand that fully, but then I was not interested in sleeping. What to do? At first there were no Sunday movies or ball games. When they came in, it was unthinkable that we children should go to such things on a Sunday. I could take a walk. I could read a good, religious book. Or I could read our denomination's Christian magazine. One of my most valuable discoveries was that the magazine had a humor column. Furthermore the people who edited it were so pure they printed some off-color jokes, the point of which they failed to see. I casually repeated the worst of them at the supper table. Mother, profoundly shocked, asked what I'd been reading. *"The Christian Observer,"* I calmly answered. I knew she would check. And when she did, the prohibition against reading the secular funny paper was quietly withdrawn.

All that is gone now. For children of the present generation, and I daresay for most of my readers, that is curious, ancient history that seems as far back in time as the landing of the Puritans at Plymouth Rock. The blue laws that kept stores and amusements closed have virtually all been repealed. Everything is wide open for whatever anyone wants to do on Sunday. Some of us still spend a couple of hours at church, but for the rest of the time, Sunday is as secular as any other day: a holiday, perhaps, but scarcely a holy day.

It has been argued that this is entirely as it should be. It was improper to take the legislation for the Jewish Sabbath on the seventh day of the week and make that binding on the Christian celebration of Jesus' resurrection on the first day of the week. We should not speak of a "Christian Sabbath" at all. Like the rest of Jewish ceremonies—the feasts, the burnt offerings, the whole system of sacrifices and so on—the Sabbath has been done away.[29]

That sounds good. I certainly do not want all the old legalisms, the inconsistent lists of what one can and cannot do on Sunday, brought back. Yet is the Sabbath principle not more than mere ceremony? I have had several experiences lately that lead me to wonder whether in getting rid of the demand of this commandment we have gotten rid of its gracious promise as well. Maybe we have thrown out the baby with the bathwater. Let me share those experiences with you and challenge you to be thinking of similar experiences you may have had.

II

One Saturday night, at an interfaith seminar, the evening was concluded by the traditional Jewish service of the end of the Sabbath. We stood in a circle and passed around a spice bag to remind ourselves to keep the fragrance of the Sabbath in our nostrils, and a cup of wine to remind us to keep the flavor of the Sabbath on our lips. Some beautiful prayers were read. Then the special Sabbath candle was plunged into the wine cup and extinguished, and the rabbi said, "The Sabbath is over." It was a moment of sweet sadness, like telling your best friend goodbye. But there was a sustaining hope—in just six days the Sabbath would come again! All of us Gentile Christians were profoundly moved and began to wonder if we were missing something.

That triggered in my mind a scene from the movie *Fiddler on the Roof.* The Sabbath comes to the little Jewish village in Czarist Russia, where most people struggle to make ends meet, suffering from unpredictable, senseless persecution from their Christian neighbors—indeed, threatened with extinction. All work stops. The best linens and dishes are put on the table. Food, prepared before sunset, is set out. The Sabbath candle is lit. The entire family, young and old, gathers. The father begins: "Blessed art thou, O Lord, creator of the universe. . . ." The camera then pans the entire village, and in every house there are windows lit with Sabbath candles. And I said to myself, "Ah! that's the secret. This is why these people in the midst of their hard lives are able to laugh and play and dance and sing." Have we been missing something?

I have been reading a book entitled *The Practice of Piety: Puritan Devotional Disciplines in Seventeenth-Century New England.* [30] Almost the first words I read there were in praise of the Sabbath. They come from a sermon by John Eliot: "A seventh part of our time is all spent in heaven, when we are duly zealous for, and zealous on the Sabbath of God. Besides, God has written on the head of the Sabbath, REMEMBER, which looks both forwards and backwards, and thus a good part of the week will be spent in sabbatizing. . . . If thou art a believer, thou art no stranger to heaven while thou livest; and when thou diest, heaven will be no strange place to thee; no, thou hast been there a thousand times before."[31] Have we been missing something?

The book on spiritual direction by Tilden Edwards, from which I drew my opening illustration, has a whole chapter entitled "The Eternal Rhythm."[32] The rhythm of most of our lives, says Edwards, is between frantic work and self-induced oblivion. On the one hand, we feel driven to create a world and a self that do not exist, that have no meaning apart from our ceaseless self-definition, toil, and work; on the other, we attempt flight into oblivion of one kind or another so we can forget the world and the self our work has made. "We fear collapse into nothingness without constant productive activity, for there is nothing apart from our activity." And we wonder why we burn out! But there is another rhythm, an eternal rhythm, says Edwards. It is the traditional Judeo-Christian rhythm of service and Sabbath, work and worship, labor and rest. We can afford to rest, and to work with eyes steadily open and hearts at peace, because our activity does not make the world or ourselves. We are held even when we do not tightly hold. There is a promise indeed! Are we missing something?

British sociologist Bruce Reed has written that the primary task of the church is to remind the culture of this rhythm. If we don't, society will soon collapse.[33]

III

Having received so many signals, I turned to the theologians of our own century to see if what I was feeling would be confirmed or squelched. I found some amazing things in Karl Barth. Barth's huge *Church Dogmatics* contains his ethics as well as his theology, and the first ethical topic treated is "The Holy Day."[34] Our human work, says Barth, is interrupted and bounded by a day on which we stop to contemplate God's work. There are indeed health considerations in the Sabbath command: we need the rest. There are public worship considerations: How would we ever get together without the Holy Day? And there are humanitarian considerations: Servants and manual workers get some protection from the Holy Day. But the real function of the Holy Day is to remind us that we are not saved by our own good works. Our work is relatively unimportant in comparison with God's work. The Sabbath strikes a deadly blow at our idolatrous worship of our own work. And so, in Barth's ethical system, it comes ahead of public confession of faith, prayer, duty to neighbor, and respect for life. Our neglect of this commandment, our refusal of this gift, is the reason our confession is not bold, our prayers are empty, our love to neighbor is cold and weak, and our respect for life wavers.

One day in class, Jürgen Moltmann asked, "What is the climax, the goal, the central purpose of the creation story with which the Bible begins?" My mouth was open to say, "The creation of human beings on the sixth day." The years have taught me that if you keep quiet, someone else will say it for you, and someone did. "No!" said Moltmann. "There are seven days in the story. And the climax, the goal, the purpose of the creation narrative is the hallowing of the Sabbath day."

Maybe Jesus was not abolishing the Sabbath, but just underlining the blessings it has for us when he said, "The sabbath was made for human beings, not human beings for the sabbath" (Mark 2:27, adapted).

IV

Much more could be said about this gracious commandment, so full of promise for us all. Let me make three quick points.

First, to obey this commandment, to claim this promise,

will make us seem strange, peculiar, different to our neighbors. This was true for ancient Israel. The most obvious differences between Israel and her neighbors were the absence of idols and the observance of the Sabbath day. Surrounding neighbors observed days set by the seasons, the moon, or the planets. But one day in seven was unheard of.

My aunt and uncle were lifelong missionaries in Korea. They were strong on the Sabbath, because Sabbath observance put an obvious public distinction between new Korean Christians and all others in their culture. I have wondered since if the astounding growth and strength of Christianity in Korea is evidence that they were right.

With the collapse of Sabbath legislation and Sabbath customs in the United States, American Christians find themselves in a position similar to Israel and the Koreans. It is not easy, particularly for children and young people, to stand out from the crowd, to be different. But if strong family support enables them to discover it can be done, what a valuable lesson they will have learned! That could be one of the hidden blessings of the Fourth Promise.

Second, the Fourth Promise is truly what Jan Lochman calls it: the Festival of Freedom.[35] It should not be divorced from its setting in the life of freed slaves. Before God's mighty and gracious act of deliverance, there was no way the slaves could get a day of rest; there was no relief from constant, unremitting toil. For them the commandment to do no work on the seventh day was a joy, a boon, an unimaginable relief. It was the most tangible reminder that they really were free at last. They could control their work time. They could choose not to work one day in seven. In the form given in Deuteronomy, this commandment reminds them to extend the same joyous freedom to those who work for them.

We have somehow got things backward. We have seen the Sabbath as an enslaving burden and asserted our freedom to work seven days a week if we want to. Few people work seven days a week at their paid jobs, but days off are devoted to yard work, housework, or the strenuous activities promoted by the recreation industry. We are still in charge, still active, still manipulating God's good creation. Very seldom are we in a hands-off posture, watching, appreciating, letting be, lost in wonder, love, and praise. We have all but forgotten how to rest.

Third, the rest this commandment promises is more than mere physical rest. It is the rest Augustine spoke of in those familiar words, "Our hearts are restless till they find their rest in Thee." We stop our work in order that God may work. Our idleness is a confession that our work is *not* more important than God's work. We take our hands off the world and wonder at it in the presence of God. Profound thinkers have always seen in the Sabbath rest a foretaste of "the saints' everlasting rest," when our employment will be the praise that surrounds the throne of God in heaven.

Here in the junkyard of our faith we have discovered a box full of treasure. It promises us a rest that the world cannot give and the world cannot take away. If we believe our suggested reading from Jeremiah, it promises us survival and prosperity for the whole people of God. How shall we open the box and claim the treasure? By remembering the Sabbath day—one day in seven, to keep it holy—different from all other days. How shall we do that in a secular culture that offers us no support? How shall we avoid falling among the legalistic thieves who robbed our ancestors of so much of the treasure? How can we get the rhythm going of doing our work and then stopping to contemplate God's work? It shouldn't be too hard, because God really wants you and me to have what's in that box!

31

The Fifth Promise: Stability

Exodus 21:15, 17
Mark 7:9–13
Ephesians 6:1–4

Honor your father and your mother, that your days may be long in the land which the LORD your God gives you.

Exodus 20:12

The ancient words ring down across the centuries: "Honor your father and your mother."

I

In one way these words sound very familiar. Here are some verbatim quotes from newspaper advertisements preceding Mother's Day:

> To Mom with love: satin loungers with Arnel for elegance
> Spring fashions to suit her fancy
> Fashionable accessories for Mom on her special day
> Bright, fresh flowers tell Mom she's special on her day
> Give Mom a treasure from the heart
> Show Mom she's number 1
> Mother's Day fragrances she'll enjoy all year round
> Cheryl Tiegs sportswear for your million-dollar Mom
> Give Mom a hand in the kitchen with handy gifts for her
> 20% off Mom's work-out bike
> Catherine's Stout Shop: remember Mom

Yes, these words are very familiar: Honor your mother in May and your father later on in June.

In another way, these are very unfamiliar words, for, newspaper advertisements and special days aside, fathers and mothers have not been highly honored among us. I know many parents who are discouraged and disheartened, filled with vain regrets and a sense of failure.

For one thing, we have been through a period of pop psychology where a child's every mental and emotional problem has been blamed on the parents. We've been told that parental tapes play in a child's mind, blighting his or her life. They've even been called "witch messages." In the lingo of Transactional Analysis, it's good to be in touch with your "OK child" and with your "adult." But you ought to avoid developing that part of your personality known as your "parent." In the older, Freudian mythology we have the Oedipus complex, in which every male child secretly wants to kill his father; and in the name of equality for the sexes, some have proposed a corresponding Electra complex for female children. Every pastor of my generation has been besieged by parents, especially in the 1960s and 1970s, asking, "Where did I go wrong?" How strange in this context to hear the ancient words, "Honor your father and your mother."

For another thing, this is the generation of parents who have been hit by the rising divorce rate in our society. The bond between father and mother has been severed. But the father is still a father, the mother is still a mother, and the children are still the children of that father and that mother. Of course, other adults often enter the constellation, bringing with them children of their former marriages, and you get stepparents and blended families and very complicated human relationships. How do we understand in all those complications the ancient words, "Honor your father and your mother"?

Yet another thing. We live today with the threat of "ageism," a prejudice against older people similar to racism and sexism. Older people used to be very few in number, highly venerated and respected just because they had managed to survive, looked up to as a source of experience and wisdom. But now that older people are increasing in numbers, they are resented if they retire because they are doing nothing, living off the social security younger workers have to pay. And if they don't retire they're resented for holding on to jobs needed by younger persons who are unemployed. Our society is intoxicated by youth. Hardly a mother in Mother's Day advertisements is over thirty. Older mothers and fathers are increasingly ridiculed, consigned to society's ash heap, resented as a reminder that we will all grow old. Yet it is clear that the Fifth Commandment originally had in mind older people, the parents of adult children who present real problems to them. The Fifth Promise is the promise of a society where older parents are supported, protected, and honored by their adult children. Thus understood, the ancient words sound strange indeed: "Honor your father and your mother."

II

What does it mean, anyway, to honor your father and your mother? It does not mean, I think, to draw a sentimental, unrealistic picture of paragons of masculine and feminine virtue that never existed. It does not mean to agree with them in all things. It does not mean undue dependence or unending immaturity.

The Bible is very blunt. In the chapter of Exodus that follows the Ten Words it says, Don't strike your father or mother; don't curse your father or mother. Some scholars, working on the theory that the Ten Words were originally uniform in style, conjecture that the original form was just that: "You will not curse your father or your mother."[36] Heavens! you say, in a civilized society we need no such admonitions. But we are learning that in our society there are many abused wives, many abused children, and, yes, many abused parents. And we are learning that the disease of abusiveness, just like alcoholism, knows no lines of social class, wealth, education, ability, age, or professed religion.

To move from the negative to the positive, Jesus taught in Mark 7 that to honor one's father and mother means to care for them, to support them financially, if needed. He said that to refuse such support, even under the guise of devoting one's money to God, is to forsake the commandment of God for human traditions.

In the suggested reading from Ephesians, a new application is made. The commandment originally designed for adult children is applied to little children in the home. To honor one's father and mother is to be obedient to them.

Checking out these biblical passages makes us aware of the changing seasons of the parent-child relationship. Often the early months and years are a time of mutual adoration. Despite the physical strain of parenting and the "terrible twos" as the child tries to assert his or her individuality, the father and mother are looked up to and honored above all other people in the child's life. Then the peer group enters the scene and the father and mother's stock slowly goes down. In the teens it hits bottom: parents are largely an embarrassment. As maturity sets in, parental stock rises a bit. You remember how Mark Twain said that when he was sixteen his father was the stupidest man he ever saw, but by the time he was twenty-one he was amazed how much the old man had learned in just five years! As the grown children become parents themselves, they begin to honor their fathers and mothers in a new way. "Did you really do all that for me?" our married daughter asked in wonder and gratitude when our first grandson was about four months old. If we work it right, there can be a long period, a good plateau, when we have an adult-to-adult relationship between children and parents. But eventually the aging process takes its toll and the children find that they must act as parents to their own parents, who are becoming increasingly childish.

Now in all these twists and turns, as best we can under the circumstances, we are to honor our parents, never treating them with contempt but with appropriate respect and gratitude. The Larger Catechism has a beautiful phrase: "bearing with their infirmities and covering them with love."

III

There are broader implications in this commandment. One is that we are to honor the past, to value the wisdom and the art of those who have gone before. Jan Lochman speaks of reverence for the tradition and community that we enter at birth. He adds that while traditional patterns cannot be given a blank check, they can be given a credit loan of critical trust.[37]

Another is that we are to honor all duly constituted authority. There are, of course, limits to that honor. Calvin says that unworthy authorities must still be honored because providence has placed them over us. But we must resist them if they lead us away from the Lord.[38] Lochman says that the Fifth Commandment must be controlled by the First and points to Acts 5:29.[39]

Still another implication is that to honor parents is to honor God. As we have seen in both the Lord's Prayer and the Apostles' Creed, two important biblical metaphors for God are parental ones: God as Father, God as Mother. And in the doctrine of the Trinity, the innermost relations within the Godhead itself are parental and filial: the love of the Father for the Son and the Son for the Father. Here the language becomes highly problematic for all of us who have become conscious of the oppressive effect of patriarchal, masculine language on women. But simple solutions, like baptizing babies in the name of the Creator, the Redeemer, and the Sanctifier miss the mark, for they leave out the parental–filial relations within the Godhead, the connection between honoring God and honoring our earthly fathers and mothers. We've got more homework to do on the problem of language about God—and the Fifth Commandment is part of that homework.

IV

It's really the Fifth Promise, of course. All the commandments, we've said, are promises. And in the Fifth Commandment the promise is very specific: "that your days may be long in the land which the LORD your God gives you."

This is the promise of stability. If you honor your father and mother, if you value and honor the past, if you give to all lawful authorities their due, if you honor and reverence God, you won't be rootless, homeless, belonging nowhere. You'll have a place.

But the promise is more to the whole people than to individuals. The nation where fathers and mothers are honored will have its place for a long time. It won't rise and fall like so many nations in history. It won't be blown off the map. Its days will be long in the land the Lord our God gives it. In this time of exponential change, of future shock, when everything we thought was nailed down is coming loose, that's a precious promise. In this day when the doomsday clock of the *Bulletin of the Atomic Scientists* stands at shortly before midnight, that's an incredible promise: stability.

This promise is not an arbitrary payoff for something unrelated—open a bank account and you get a toaster—the promise is inherent in the commandment. As Andrew Greeley says, "In a society without compassion for the aged, there will not be enough trust or respect for the society to persist long."[40] On the other hand, a society in which fathers and mothers are honored and respected, in which their infirmities are covered over with love, is a stable society, the kind of society where families can put down roots and where national catastrophe can be avoided.

"Honor your father and your mother, that your days may be long in the land which the LORD your God gives you."

32

The Sixth Promise:
Life

Genesis 4:8–10
John 10:7–10

You will not kill.
   Exodus 20:13

We have been saying of the Ten Words that they may be read as prohibitions—"You must not kill"—or they may be read as promises—"You will not kill."

I

Surely nothing is simpler than to read the Sixth Word as a prohibition: you must not kill, not ever, under any circumstances. Since the day Cain killed his brother, Abel, we have known that nothing is more clearly wrong than taking another human life. It is wrong, as Calvin points out, because all killing is the killing of our own flesh, since all human beings are brothers and sisters. Furthermore, it is wrong because all human beings are made in the image of God, so an assault against a human brother or sister is an assault against God.[41] It is wrong, says Walter Harrelson, because human life belongs to God. To take human life is to assume the prerogatives of God![42]

Yet when you read comments on this commandment—in the ancient catechisms, in modern church pronouncements, in writings of ethicists and theologians—nothing seems more complicated. Once this word is seen as a prohibition, a rule, the search begins for exceptions to the rule. And plenty of them are found.

You must not kill, *except* in self-defense. When it's him or me, it's OK to kill him—or her, as the case may be.

You must not kill, *except* in war. When it's us or the Germans (or the Japanese, or the Russians), it's OK to kill them.

You must not kill, *except* in capital punishment. In order to protect law-abiding citizens, it's OK for the state to kill criminals.

And you can find biblical texts, mostly in the Old Testament, telling with apparent approval of killing in self-defense and even ordering, in the name of God, killing in war and capital punishment. The same book that says, "You must not kill," says, "Yes, but there are times when you must."

It is evident that to discuss the Sixth Word as a prohibition is to become involved in the most controversial issues of our day, of any day—war and capital punishment, but also suicide, abortion, and euthanasia. As you read on in the discussions of this commandment you may encounter such matters as medical experimentation on human bodies, pollution of the environment, gun control, birth control, sterilization, and so on.

It is almost impossible to find agreement or consistency among Christians on these issues. There are Christians who say abortion is always wrong because to them it is killing a human being, yet many of them tend to approve of capital punishment and war. There are other Christians who feel abortion has a rightful place because to them it is not killing, yet many of them would say capital punishment is always wrong. As to war, there are total pacifists, nuclear pacifists, and advocates of peace through strength.

No, the Sixth Word as prohibition is far from simple. It is terribly complex. We find it difficult to be consistent about it, impossible to give answers in advance of a specific case. Maybe the best we can do is to follow the procedure outlined in the thoughtful report on "The Nature and

Value of Human Life," adopted by the 1981 General Assembly of the Presbyterian Church, U.S. The Sixth Commandment, says that report, commands both that we do no harm to human life and that we do all we can to protect it. In many cases, in order to protect some human life we have to harm other human life. In each instance we ask, Will the harm done outweigh the protection achieved, or will the protection achieved outweigh the harm done?

But even that is not simple, for we must remember that our judgment will be skewed by our sinfulness and self-interest, and that we are not omniscient; we don't always know how to predict either the harm or the protection. Long before the recent treaty regarding intermediate-range nuclear missiles, I had the opportunity to discuss that great threat to human life with a high official of the Russian Orthodox Church. I pointed out to him that many members of American churches had opposed the deployment of the Cruise and Pershing II missiles in Europe. I asked if there had been any opposition in his church to the deployment of SS-20 missiles by the Soviet government. He responded with about five minutes of nonstop, heated Russian, which when it was translated and boiled down amounted to this: The Cruise and Pershing II missiles are threats to human life and therefore violate the Sixth Commandment. But the SS-20 missiles are a defense of human life and therefore fulfill the Sixth Commandment. I'm afraid all of us, at one time or another, are swayed like that by our own self-interest in trying to interpret the Sixth Word as commandment.

II

Let's see if it will help to read this as the Sixth Promise. "I have delivered you, and I will be your God and you will be my people. Therefore, you will not kill. You will become a human community in which it is no longer necessary to kill, either in self-defense, or in capital punishment, or in war."

Fantasize with me a disarmed community. There is so

much p-e-a-c-e that you don't have to carry a p-i-e-c-e. Many little children in the ghetto feel they must carry a piece—a knife or some other weapon—in order to get across the ghetto and back alive. But in the disarmed community, no one needs a knife or a gun. The state does not need an electric chair or a gas chamber. Nations do not need smart bombs or conventional weapons. Swords have been beaten into plowshares, spears into pruning hooks. Nation does not lift up sword against nation, neither do they study war any more. Each family sits under its own vine and its own fig tree with none to make them afraid (Micah 4:1–4). That's a picture of the Sixth Promise!

An impossible dream? But it is God's dream for us. It is God's chosen future. It is the way God wants it to be. And to live the Christian life is to live from that future, not from all the darkness of the past, all the past murders and executions and wars, even the biblical ones. To live the Christian life is to live as though that future is now, as citizens of the kingdom of God even while we are still citizens of the present evil age. The heart of the good news Jesus proclaimed was "The kingdom of God is at hand!" The promised future is right out there, so close you can reach out and put your hand on it! Begin to live in it now!

This is a high-risk procedure, not for the fearful or fainthearted. You could get yourself killed trying to do it. But you would not enter the next life with someone else's blood on your hands.

Let us freely admit that it is not necessarily easier to be consistent about the Sixth Promise than about the Sixth Commandment. Our fantasies about the promise may not agree more closely than did our divergent interpretations of the rule.

But I think that, if we lived by the promise, the sort of uncritical acceptance of war and blessing of war that has marked the church since the time of Constantine would go. The uncritical acceptance of any kind of killing would go. Any taking of human life would be, as Karl Barth describes it, an extreme exception on the farthest edge of the most desperate circumstances.[43]

The center of our attention would be not on the exceptions but on what furthers the promise, what makes for life. Not in asking, Under what circumstances would I be justified in killing in self-defense? but, How can I defend myself without killing? Not, Under what circumstances would my nation be justified in going to war? but, How can my nation defend itself and its values without war? Not, Under what circumstances is capital punishment justified? but, How can we deal with crime without capital punishment? Not, Under what circumstances is an abortion permissible? but, How can we handle our sexuality as men and women so that abortion is not needed as a way out? Not, When is euthanasia proper? but, How can health care and medical treatment be carried out so that it is not called for? How can we build a society that does not breed aggression or war or crime or oppression of women or brutalizing pain or despair?

Jesus said he came that we might have life and have it abundantly (John 10:10). As followers of Jesus, that is our primary relation to the Sixth Word: champions of life; workers with God for abundant life in this world; living at risk, as though the future belongs to God and to us and to all living things; every day making that future a present reality as far as we can.

That sounds like fun to me!

33

The Seventh Promise: Faithfulness

Jeremiah 5:8; 9:2; 13:27; 23:10
1 Corinthians 6:12–20

You will not commit adultery.
Exodus 20:14

The first seven promises say that if we can ever get the covenant really operating—"I will be your God and you will be my people"—this is the way it will be: you will have no other gods, you will not worship idols, you will not misuse the divine name, you will not forget the Holy Day, you will not dishonor parents, you will not kill, and you will not commit adultery. This last is not an easy promise to grasp in our day and time.

I

Let us sneak up on it by the most time-honored of flank attacks, the birds and the bees. Television offers us many programs of stunning wildlife photography. In almost all of them you see the enormous strength of the drive to mate and procreate. We human animals share that drive. In some animals mating creates no lasting bond; the male wanders off, leaving the female the whole task of birthing and rearing the young. In others, mating creates a temporary bond; the pair work together until the young are old enough to make it on their own. In a third group, mating creates a lifelong bond, a bond of lasting faithfulness.

I think it can be safely said that the high purpose of God for humankind is to include us in that third group. God's purpose for us is that sexual union should create a lifelong bond of faithfulness. But God did not program us for that with instincts we would automatically obey. God created human sexuality as an amazingly complex thing. And God gave us human freedom.

So God's high purpose for us has been honored as much in the breach as in the observance. Adultery may be defined as a breach of that high purpose: having mated with one, to wander off and mate with another and perhaps another and another, often secretly and deceptively behind the first partner's back.

In how many novels is adultery the theme? Remove adultery and how many plays and operas would be left? How many poems are confessions of adulterous love? How much history is the story of royal adulteries? How many stories in the Bible concern adulteries: Abraham with Hagar, Judah with Tamar, Potiphar's wife's attempt on Joseph, David with Bathsheba, Hosea's wife with who knows?

In much great literature, certainly in the Bible, adultery is recognized as wrong, as falling short of God's high purpose for us. But there are times in history when adultery seems to be accepted as the norm and lifelong faithfulness is ridiculed. Jeremiah lived in such a time.

> O that I had in the desert
>   a wayfarers' lodging place,
> that I might leave my people
>   and go away from them!
> For they are all adulterers,
> a company of treacherous men. . . .
> They are well-fed lusty stallions,
>   each neighing for his neighbor's wife. . . .
> I have seen your abominations,
>   your adulteries and neighings, your lewd harlotries,
>   on the hills in the field.

> Woe to you, O Jerusalem!
> How long will it be
> before you are made clean? . . .
> The land is full of adulterers.
> Jeremiah 9:2; 5:8; 13:27; 23:10

Jesus lived in such a time. He speaks frequently of "this sinful and adulterous generation." It seems to me that we live in such a time. Public figures are openly adulterous and everyone applauds; their popularity is not diminished. Heroes and heroines of TV shows are expected to have an adulterous affair on the side; they are not authentic without that. The implication, not lost on our children, is that adultery is normal, right, glamorous, and to be imitated.

Listen to a recent radio talk show. Male speaker: "People can say things like 'I'm crazy about tennis' or 'I'm wild about golf.' Why can't we say 'I'm crazy about sex. I'm wild about it anytime, anywhere, with anybody'?" Female speaker (apparently a psychologist): "Fortunately there are more and more circles where it is acceptable for you to talk that way. But unfortunately there are still people whose parents gave them the wrong view of sex or who have been messed up by church and religion and that kind of thing."

I can seldom understand the words of rock singers with all that other noise going on. But those who have cracked the code tell me that the music makers regularly feed young people with open invitations to promiscuous sex.

In such a culture at such a time, the Seventh Commandment is a laughingstock. And the Seventh Promise, that life will be marked by faithfulness, does not seem very desirable. Who wants faithfulness when unfaithfulness is so fashionable and such fun?

II

Nevertheless, it is possible that in the Seventh Commandment and the Seventh Promise we may not be dealing simply with outmoded Victorianism. We may be dealing with realities about our humanity, about the way we were created, which this sinful and adulterous generation has forgotten but which the Bible still remembers.

I invite your attention to our suggested New Testament passage, 1 Corinthians 6:12–20. In talking about human freedom and its limitations, Paul sets forth a dynamic view of sex. The whole body, the whole self, comes to a focus in sexual union, so that the most casual kind of adultery, consorting with prostitutes, is nonetheless a giving of self so profound that the adulterer and the prostitute become one body. We recognize this dynamism of sex in common speech. "I must have her." "How many men have you had?" That is strong language of ownership, possession, union—the giving and taking of selves.

The only comparable dynamic relationship is religious conversion, where we give ourselves to Christ, become one body with Christ, have him and he has us. If this is true, what happens to us when we give ourselves away in adulterous relationships as casually as we give away pennies? What happens to us when we take the bodies, the selves of others, as casually as picking flowers in a garden? We become incapable of faithfulness: faithfulness to other people and faithfulness to God.

Now perhaps we are prepared to appreciate the wonder of the Seventh Promise. "If you will be my people, I will be your God and you will not commit adultery. There will be no unfaithfulness among you. Despite the strength of your sexual drives, you will not succumb to an unfaithful use of sex. Despite the fashionableness of unfaithfulness, you will remain faithful. And so you will be spared the fragmentation, the jealousy, the suspicion, the lies, the deceitfulness, the selfishness, the godlessness that mark your culture and your generation." Every soap opera I have looked at is essentially a web of lies, of betrayals, of deceit, of unfaithfulness. To be part of a community that is free from that is a royal promise indeed!

III

How shall we help our young people and the generations to come after them? I am convinced we shall not move out of the sexual morass of our day by commandments and prohibitions and rules and more rules; young people have always been expert at getting around rules. We shall move out by a shining vision of what human faithfulness can be. To know that you belong fully to another human being whom you love; to know that that person belongs fully to you; to live together, free from suspicion and jealousy, not because you're both strong and perfect, but because you both belong fully to God, who forgives your past and keeps you faithful into the future—there's a vision to make the spine tingle and the heart beat faster and the eyes shine.

Remember the time-honored words, "In the Name of God, I take you to be my wife, to be my husband, to have and to hold from this day forward, for better, for worse, for richer, for poorer, in sickness and in health, to love and to cherish, until we are parted by death. This is my promise." It is not just the groom's promise or the bride's promise that is involved. It is God's promise.

IV

One problem with any discussion of the Seventh Commandment is that, strictly interpreted, it does not include us all. It applies only to married people, since adultery, strictly interpreted, is a breach of the marriage relationship. There is, however, a word of Jesus that makes it inclusive. "You have heard that it was said, 'You shall not commit adultery.' But I say to you that every one who looks at a woman lustfully has already committed adultery with her in his heart" (Matt. 5:27–28). Assuming that for women to look lustfully at men is also implied, we are now all included, are we not? We are all adulterers and stand under the commandment; that's the bad news. But we all stand under the promise, and that's the good news. "A Declaration of Faith" puts it this way:

> God intends all people—
>   whether children, youth, or adults,
>   single, divorced, married, or widowed—
>   to affirm each other as males and females
>   with joy, freedom, and responsibility.
> We confess the value of love and faithfulness
>   and the disaster of lust and faithlessness
>   in all our associations as women and men.[44]

The promise is not restricted. And the promise is not too late. Despite the "new morality" described earlier, there are many despairing people who see themselves as fallen men or ruined women. Let us say this clearly, so no one may miss it: Adultery is not the unforgivable sin. Once a group of religious men brought to Jesus a woman who had been caught in the very act of adultery. After he shamed the accusers and they all left, Jesus turned to the woman. "Has no one condemned you?" "No one, Lord." "Neither do I condemn you; go, and do not sin again" (John 7:53–8:11). That's good news. That's part of the Seventh Promise.

Regardless of the past, from this time on, you will not commit adultery. Regardless of the past, from this time on, a life of faithfulness is open to you. Thank God for the Seventh Promise!

34

The Eighth Promise: Generosity

Leviticus 19:9–10
Ephesians 4:28

You will not steal.
    Exodus 20:15

Many biblical scholars think that the original form of the commandment was: "You shall not steal a human being" (compare Ex. 21:16; Deut. 24:7). This would make it not a prohibition of stealing in general but a specific prohibition of kidnapping, of capturing persons to sell them into slavery. One reason the scholars give for this interpretation is that a blanket prohibition on stealing seems aimed at the poor. The Bible is on the side of the poor and encourages them to take for themselves the grain in the corners of the rich farmer's field, the gleanings of the harvest, the olives left on the tree, the grapes left on the vine (compare Lev. 19:9–10; Deut. 24:19–22; the book of Ruth).

But stealing can be from above as well as from below.[45] The Eighth Commandment was given not only for the protection of the "haves" but also for the protection of the "have nots." It is in connection with this commandment that Calvin condemns "harsh and inhuman laws with which the more powerful crush and oppress the weak."[46]

It seems to me, then, right and proper to treat the Eighth Commandment as it has traditionally been treated, as a prohibition of stealing in general, whether from below or from above, whether by the "have nots" or the "haves." Of course the stealing of persons is the most serious form of stealing. In addition to kidnapping and slavery, economic practices that rob people of their very livelihood, lead them to "sell their souls to the company store," and immobilize them by indebtedness may be considered "stealing human beings." Such practices are far more serious than thefts that take from people luxuries and superfluities that can easily be replaced.

I

What is going on in our society? We have been characterized as the Now Generation, the Pepsi Generation, the Lite Generation, as in "lite" beer, "lite" wine, "lite" cigarettes. Would you believe the Stealing Generation?

The amount of theft in our day and time staggers the imagination. We read that one in four Americans will be a victim of crime each year, and the majority of those crimes will be thefts. The elderly poor will have their Social Security checks stolen or will be mugged as they leave the bank with the cash. The middle class and the wealthy will have their homes burglarized or their cars stolen. Retail stores will figure on losses from shoplifting and pass the costs on to their more honest customers. Information will be stolen from computer networks, programming from cable TV companies, communion ware from churches. The U.S. government, and we the taxpayers, will be bilked of *$50 billion,* according to the government's own Private Sector Cost Control Panel, most of that not by welfare cheats but by so-called reputable corporations. And our entire generation will be stealing from our grandchildren by squandering earth's irreplaceable resources and accumulating a monetary deficit that cannot be repaid in the foreseeable future.

So we have become also the Self-Protective Generation. Some citizens never leave their apartments for fear of being robbed; they are jailed by their own possessions. The sale of dead-bolt locks and electronic surveillance systems is booming. Watchdogs—the meaner the better—are in vogue. One bumper sticker reads, THE KEYS ARE ON THE FRONT SEAT, RIGHT BY THE DOBERMAN. Churches are no longer open for prayer.

Surely it is a voice from another world that we hear saying, "You will not steal." It is a command, to be sure: "As God's people you are expected not to steal." But it is also a promise: "As God's people, what God has in store for you is an impossible possibility, a redeemed human community where people will not steal." Let your mind savor that vision: a community without dead-bolt locks, without people imprisoned in their own apartments; no terrible suspicion of strangers; no ripping off of stores or the government or our own grandchildren.

On a recent vacation my wife and I had a delightful surprise. We checked into a church conference center and stood at the desk waiting for our room key. "There are no keys," said the desk clerk, "no one has to lock." The Eighth Promise encourages us to dream of a whole society where that could be true. It seems impossible. Yet not only Don Quixote but all God's people are called on to dream the impossible dream.

II

Why do people steal?

Some steal because they are hungry. Victor Hugo's great novel *Les Miserables* is about Jean Valjean, a simple vineyard pruner in rural France, the only support of his widowed sister and five children, who lost his job. In desperation, to feed the hungry children, he stole a loaf of bread from a bakery and was sentenced to row in the galleys in chains. Because of repeated attempts to escape, his sentence totaled nineteen years.

Some people steal because they are addicted. Addicts steal to feed a different kind of hunger. It takes over $100 a day to support a heroin habit. An addicted gambler needs large sums. Easy credit has addicted many people to unrealistic lifestyles.

Some people steal for kicks, as a sort of game. Much shoplifting is done by young people whose parents can buy them all they need. But they get a kick out of beating the system, bragging to their friends about what they have done. Their parents may do something similar on income taxes, expense accounts, or insurance claims for damages.

Some people steal for greed. The professionals who steal silverware and melt it down on the truck, or who steal automobiles and "chop" them for parts, are not hungry or addicted or out for kicks. They are greedy for the money it will bring. The growers who stopped enforcement of the hard-won gains of the Farm Workers Union are not hungry. They are greedy. When major defense contractors sell the Air Force 29-cent transistors for $112; when they bill the Pentagon $2,518 per hour for $10-per-hour production workers; when they sell the Navy $15 claw hammers for $435 and the Air Force 12-cent allen wrenches for $9,609, their executives are not hungry. They are greedy. They will plead that they do not pocket the money; they are under pressure from their stockholders to maximize profits. Then their stockholders are greedy. This is stealing from above, but neither the stockholders nor the executives will go to the galleys.

III

If such things are the causes of stealing, what can bring about a society where the Eighth Commandment is obeyed and the Eighth Promise fulfilled? How deeply entrenched, seemingly insoluble, are the problems of hunger and addiction and gamesmanship and greed! Only a miracle of God can bring this about.

I began to sense the shape of that miracle when I stumbled across our suggested reading from Ephesians. "Let the thief no longer steal"—that's a realistic beginning. Not "no Christian should ever steal," for in one way or another we have all stolen. But, as a community of ex-thieves, "no more stealing—steal no longer." And what will change us and cure us and bring about the miracle? Not a program we can fashion. What can change us is what Thomas Chalmers called "the expulsive power of a new affection." Listen to the rest of the text, put in the plural to include us all: "Let the thieves no longer steal, but rather let them labor, doing honest work with their hands, so that they may be able to give to those in need."

Giving is a positive addiction that is stronger than all the negative addictions that lead to stealing. Giving is a thrill that makes gambling seem tame. Giving is a kick that makes heroin seem a drag. Giving is an excitement that makes shoplifting seem dull. Giving is one thing that is stronger than greed!

Giving rules out stealing. I can't give what is not mine. If I give what I have stolen, the real giver is the person from whom I stole. In order to be able to give to those in need, I must labor, I must do honest work, so that what I give is truly mine to give.

The society where "you will not steal" is, quite simply, a generous society. Generosity is catching. Jean Valjean receives the incredible generosity of the bishop who gives him the silver he was attempting to steal. In turn he becomes the generous benefactor of many others. Even the bishop's generosity cannot compare with God's generosity toward us. God spared not the only Son but delivered him up for us all and with him freely gives us all things (Rom. 8:32). When we let that generosity make us generous, the Eighth Promise will begin to be fulfilled among us.

35

The Ninth Promise: Truthfulness

Psalm 15
Ephesians 4:22–25

You will not bear false witness
against your neighbor.

Exodus 20:16

The Ten Commandments are also Ten Promises. That's what we've been saying in each chapter. Recently another word has been coming into our discussions: "dreams." These are God's Ten Dreams for us. Human parents have high dreams for their children. So does the divine Parent.

God dreams of a community, bound by covenant to God and to one another, where there will be no killing and no adultery and no stealing. Impossible dreams—but we have tried with great effort to wrap our minds around them, to dream along with God.

But when God dreams of a covenant community in which there is no lying, how can we dream along? Who can conceive of a community that is totally free from deceit, falsehood, slander, flattery, lies?

I

Actually, in the Ninth Word, God starts off rather modestly. "I have a dream," says God, "that I will be your God and you will be my people, and in that community you wil¹ not bear false witness against your neighbor."

The setting is clearly a place where testimony is taken and witness is borne. A court of law comes to mind, but a committee hearing, a performance evaluation, a letter of recommendation, even a letter to the editor or a newspaper report could also qualify. There you will not be false. We all sense that to lie when the reputation or the job or the freedom or the life of a person is at stake would be a violation of the Ninth Commandment. We may not be so sure about an idle tale at a social gathering.

Again, it is *malicious* lying that is forbidden: false witness *against* the neighbor. We all sense that it is far worse to tell lies that injure someone than to tell lies designed to help someone. Whoever went through childhood and the teens without lying to keep a friend out of trouble with teachers and parents? Tom Sawyer lied to save Becky Thatcher from getting a licking and took the licking himself. Becky's father, Judge Thatcher, called it "a noble lie." And what do we say about lies designed to help people in a profound way? In *Les Miserables* the bishop's generosity to Jean Valjean involved a noble lie. The bishop had taken Jean in for the night. Jean awoke, stole all the bishop's silver, and fled. The gendarmes caught him and brought him back to the bishop. Without hesitation the bishop said, "I gave you the candlesticks also, which are silver like the rest. Why did you not take them along with your plates?" That, of course, was the redeeming moment in the life of Jean Valjean. It pursues him throughout the entire novel. In the movie *Places of the Heart*, almost the identical redemptive lie cements the healing relationship between Sally Field and the black farmer who wanders into her home in a little Texas town during the Depression. Do these lies violate the Ninth Commandment?

Once again, it is the *neighbor* against whom we should not lie. We all sense it is worse to be false in dealing with those close to us and dependent on us than in dealing with an enemy or a tyrant. When Dietrich Bonhoeffer pretended to be working for the Nazi government while he was actually plotting its overthrow, was that a violation of the Ninth Commandment?

Already we've said enough to see why this it the most tangled area of ethics. Ethicists disagree on what constitutes a lie and on whether lies are always wrong. All the discussions are full of exceptions, nuances, qualifications. Situation ethics was born out of the struggle to determine what really constitutes a lie.

II

Let's try another tack. Let's turn again to that remarkable chapter in Ephesians where the commandments get restated positively and with new motivations. Ephesians 4:25 speaks of "putting away falsehood": that is, not trying to define it, or to rank it as bad, worse, and worst; not letting it be the center of attention. It goes on to say, "Speak the truth," and the original makes it clear that we are to speak it continuously, constantly, habitually. Not only in court but everywhere and every day; not just refraining from the damaging falsehood, but positively, enthusiastically speaking the truth. Truth narrowly defined as simply the agreement of words with facts can doubtless at times be mean and selfish and destructive. But truth as the Bible uses it—being real, genuine, faithful to your promises, *being* true—is always upbuilding and healing and redeeming, even when it is difficult, risky, and painful.

All the catechisms of the church interpret the Ninth Word in the light of Ephesians and similar New Testament passages. The Larger Catechism speaks of "appearing and standing for the truth; and from the heart, sincerely, freely, clearly, and fully, speaking the truth, and only the truth, in matters of judgment and justice, and in all other things whatsoever" (Question 144).

Now for the new motivation, so typical of Ephesians: "Let every one speak the truth with his or her neighbor, for we are members one of another." The image here is the familiar one of the Body of Christ. As Christ's covenant people we belong to each other; we depend on each other, just as the organs of a human body are interdependent. If my head aches, I ache all over. If my stomach is nauseated, I'm sick all over. If someone rubs my aching back, I feel good all over. "If one member suffers, all suffer together; if one member is honored, all rejoice together" (1 Cor. 12:26). To lie in that situation is to poison the whole body, including yourself, with untruth. To tell the truth is to release light and healing into the whole body, including yourself.

III

Let us reflect on two areas where truth-telling is important. First is the intimate area, in families and friendships. It is amazing how often people settle down to patterns of untruth in their most intimate relationships, how they live lies. Both parties may know what the truth is, but they dare not bring it to speech, for fear of hurting the other or for fear of revealing themselves. So they play games. For years they may play destructive, corrupting games.

One way to understand what good counseling and good therapy are all about is to see that their aim is to help us tell the truth. The counselor listens to the partial truths we pour out. Just listening is helpful and healing. But somewhere by a question or a raised eyebrow the counselor will express a difference, will suggest subtly or bluntly, "That's not the whole truth." That's the point where we begin to get angry with our counselors. But if we hang in and work, we come to the moment of truth. "So that's what I've been doing! And that's who I've been doing it with. And that's who I've been doing it to! Will I now risk the pain to myself and to the others of bringing the truth to speech?" Telling the truth makes it possible for the first time to do what our scripture says: to put off the old nature, corrupt through deceitful lusts, and put on the new nature, created after the image of God in the righteousness and holiness that come from truth.

IV

A second area where truth-telling is important is the public arena: politics. We joke about all politicians being liars, but we want above all else to trust our government, to believe that our leaders are telling us the truth.

I believed that, in spite of everything, because I wanted to so badly, until I read *The Pentagon Papers* in 1972. There they were: the official documents, showing our leaders discussing how to deceive the American public, making preparations for the very things they were saying publicly they would never do. I was physically ill. So I can understand those who still cling, against all evidence, to a tenacious belief that those who govern us surely will not deceive us, propagandize us, manipulate us.

In the years since 1972, truth has not fared well in government. Trust in our leaders erodes more and more. Polls show that the majority believe our leaders to be lying. But there is little if any moral outrage. There is a numbed acceptance that this is the way it is: most people are liars.

I think the Ninth Commandment bids us in a situation like this to tell the truth constantly, unceasingly—even when those who want so desperately to believe in their government won't listen to us; even if the government attempts to use its considerable power to silence us; even if it seems disloyal. The supreme act of loyalty is to tell the truth, no matter what the risk or pain. The Larger Catechism says that one of the sins forbidden by the Ninth Commandment is "undue silence in a just cause" (Question 145).

My dream, says God, is a community where my people always tell the upbuilding, healing, redemptive truth. We're a long way from there. I don't know when God's dream will ever come true. But I do know that every time we bring the truth to speech, in intimate relationships or in public affairs, we move a little nearer to God's dream.

And every time we keep silent to protect ourselves from risk and pain, we move nearer to a terrible nightmare that God does not choose. No parent would choose that nightmare for his or her children. Let us dare to dream God's impossible dream!

36

The Tenth Promise:
Contentment

1 Kings 21
Philippians 4:11–13

You will not covet your neighbor's house; you will not
covet your neighbor's wife, or his manservant, or his maidservant, or his ox, or his ass, or anything that is your neighbor's.

Exodus 20:17

In our discussions of the Ten Commandments, we've
tried to treat them positively, as God's promises, God's
dreams of what human community can be like. God
dreams of a community where there is no murder, but
rather profound respect for human life; of a community
where there is no adultery, but rather commitment and
faithfulness; of a community where there is no stealing,
but rather generosity; of a community where there is no
lying, but rather truthfulness. Now the final dream: a community where there is no covetousness, but rather contentment.

I

What is covetousness? Stories are often better than def-
initions, and the story found in the Old Testament reading
I have suggested (1 Kings 21) will show us what it is.

King Ahab, who had his palace and plenty of land and servants galore, wanted something more. He wanted a vineyard that belonged to his neighbor Naboth. He wanted it very badly. He tried to buy it from Naboth, or to trade him other land for it, but Naboth refused. There was an ancient idea in Israel that every family should keep the land originally assigned them when Canaan was first conquered. This way there would never develop a permanent underclass of landless people. In the legislation for the Year of Jubilee (Leviticus 25), which may never have been enforced, the land had to go back to the original owners every fifty years. That set a time limit on the process whereby the rich get richer and the poor get poorer. Naboth, out of loyalty to that ancient tradition, refused to part with his family's land. Ahab, sick with desire for it, went to bed, stared at the wall, and refused to eat. His wife, Jezebel, took matters into her own hands, had Naboth killed, and invited Ahab to go down and look over his new property. But there stood Elijah with God's word of severe condemnation for Ahab's covetousness.

Covetousness is the desire for what our neighbor has when we already have enough. Covetousness is the refusal ever to be satisfied with what we have. Someone has said that in our affluent American society "enough is always more." That in a nutshell is covetousness.

It would have been equally appropriate to illustrate covetousness from the story of David in 2 Samuel 11–12. David, who had many wives, coveted Bathsheba, the wife of Uriah the Hittite. He sent and took her and then tried to cover up what he had done by bringing Uriah home from the army. Uriah refused to go home to his wife, so David had him killed. This time it was Nathan the prophet who brought God's word of condemnation.

God says to Ahab, It is wrong to covet your neighbor's real estate. God says to David, It is wrong to covet your neighbor's wife. God says to us all, It is wrong to covet anything that is your neighbor's; it is wrong to build a society where enough is always more.

II

The Tenth Commandment is different from the other nine. They deal chiefly with external conduct, outward behavior. We can at least imagine obeying them, even if we feel very differently inside: refraining from murder, even though we're full of anger; refraining from adultery, even though we're full of lust; refraining from perjury, even though our hearts are deceitful; and so on.

In the Sermon on the Mount, Jesus internalized those commandments. It was said, don't murder; but I say, don't be full of anger and contempt. It was said, don't commit adultery; but I say, don't look at another human being to lust after that person. But Jesus did not have to deepen or internalize the Tenth Commandment, because it already goes deep, it is already internal. As the Larger Catechism says, it deals with our "inward motions and affections" (Question 147). In the Tenth Commandment the Old Testament comes close to the New; Moses shakes hands with Jesus!

Covetousness is not confined to inward motions and affections. Scholars tell us that the Hebrew word for "covet" involves not only desire for something that is rightfully the neighbor's, but planning and scheming and trying to get it. We certainly see that in the stories of Naboth and David. But covetousness begins in the heart, and we cannot control it the way we may be able to control outward actions. There is no way we can hold our breath, tug at our bootstraps, and say, "I will not covet." Only an inner transformation wrought by God can bring that about.

III

Covetousness is the enemy of personal peace. We cannot be quiet and serene within if our hearts are eaten up with the desire for things that are not ours.

Covetousness is the enemy of peace in the family. How many of us have seen families torn and divided when the patriarch or matriarch dies and the will is read and each child covets something that went to a brother or sister or to some charity?

Covetousness is the enemy of peace in the church. Most church lawsuits are over property. When congregations are divided, the central question is, usually, Who shall retain ownership of the building?

Covetousness is the enemy of peace in the community. Who shall have use of the land: the throughway, the residents, or the developers? See you in court!

Covetousness is the enemy of peace in the nation. There can be no real national peace as long as covetous business interests offer tempting bounties to the Congress and covetous public officials accept them, while the neglected poor sink ever deeper into poverty.

Covetousness is the enemy of peace in the world. Third-world countries devote land and human energy—that should be used to feed their own people—to the production of coffee and bananas, lumber and minerals for the first and second worlds. So the covetousness of the "haves" robs the "have-nots" of the basic necessities of life. It is not too great a simplification to say that the first and second worlds are locked in a struggle for raw materials from the third world that they need for their industrial machines. That is a significant part of the rivalry that imperils the future of our planet.

The writer of James saw this long ago. "What causes wars, and what causes fightings among you? Is it not your passions [TEV, desires for pleasure] that are at war in your members? You desire and do not have; so you kill. And you covet and cannot obtain; so you fight and wage war" (James 4:1–2).

I remember a moving sermon by Gardner Taylor, the pastor of the Concord Baptist Church in Brooklyn. His text was the valley of dry bones in Ezekiel 37. He described the situation in the United States as seen from the viewpoint of the black community: soaring unemployment among youth, high rents, decaying buildings, streets, bridges, sidewalks, the lack of law enforcement, the unavailability of health care, the disastrous effects of the drug trade, the

corruption of public officials, a foreign policy that be-
friends military dictators and the oppressors of black people. "What is behind all this?" he asked. After a long pause,
he rolled out one word like a peal of thunder: "Greed!" In
that moment I heard the plain, eloquent English for covetousness. It is *greed.* After another silence Dr. Taylor repeated his text: "Son of man, can these bones live?" "O
Lord GOD, thou knowest."

IV

God knows and cares. And God promises. The promise
is the end of greed. Stated positively, the promise is contentment.

Years ago, when I taught at Stillman College, they had
a marvelous yell they used at basketball games. When a
Stillman Tiger dropped one through the basket, the stands
would erupt with: *(clap, clap, clap)* "Satisfied!" *(clap, clap,
clap)* "Satisfied!" *(clap, clap, clap)* "Satisfied!" God
dreams of a community where people accept their blessings with a constant cheer: *(clap, clap, clap)* "Satisfied!"

In what must be one of the most gracious thank-you
notes ever written, the letter to the Philippians, the apostle Paul expresses contentment unforgettably: "I know
how to be abased, and I know how to abound; in any and
all circumstances I have learned the secret of facing plenty
and hunger, abundance and want. I can do all things in
him who strengthens me" (Phil. 4:12–13,). For Paul the
promise had come true: "You will not covet."

John Woolman, the Quaker tailor in colonial times
whom I have mentioned before, learned the same secret.

> My mind, through the power of truth, was in a good degree
> weaned from the desire of outward greatness, and I was
> learning to be content with real conveniences, that were
> not costly, so that a way of life free from much entangle-
> ment appeared best for me, though the income might be
> small. I had several offers of business that appeared profit-

able, but I did not see my way clear to accept of them, believing they would be attended with more outward care and cumber than was required of me to engage in. I saw that an humble man, with the blessing of the Lord, might live on a little, and that where the heart was set on greatness, success in business did not satisfy the craving; but that commonly with an increase of wealth the desire of wealth increased. There was a care on my mind so to pass my time that nothing might hinder me from the most steady attention to the voice of the true Shepherd."[47]

Woolman's *Journal* is studded with subsequent references to his efforts to reduce the volume of his business and to live more simply in order that he might have more time for the great concern that the true Shepherd had laid on his heart: the abolition of slavery. It was his conviction that if the colonists would live simply and be content with real conveniences, they would not need to buy slaves, they would not need to cheat the Indians out of more land, they would not need to maintain armies and fight wars.

We need to be careful when we talk about contentment. Oppressors have used the idea of contentment as a tool of oppression. I remember all too well the days of the civil rights struggle when segregationists kept telling me that black people were quite content with second-class citizenship. "Give them enough watermelon and they're perfectly happy." It was "outside agitators," they said, who were causing all the trouble. There are situations where justice requires discontent. It is never proper for the "haves" to say to the "have-nots," "You must be content." God's dream is not that the oppressed will be content with oppression, but that those who have enough will be content with what they have.

V

There is a bond between contentment and love that John Calvin, among others, was quick to see.

The purpose of this commandment is: since God wills that our whole soul be possessed with a disposition to love, we must banish from our hearts all desire contrary to love. To sum up, then: no thought should steal upon us to move our hearts to a harmful covetousness that tends to our neighbor's loss. To this corresponds the opposite precept: whatever we conceive, deliberate, will, or attempt is to be linked to our neighbor's good and advantage. . . .

For who can deny that it is right for all the powers of the soul to be possessed with love? But if any soul wander from the goal of love, who will not admit that it is diseased? Now how does it happen that desires hurtful to your brother enter your heart, unless it is that you disregard him and strive for yourself alone? For if your whole heart were steeped in love, not one particle of it would lie open to such imaginings. The heart, then, in so far as it harbors covetousness, must be empty of love.[48]

The First Commandment or Promise, "You will have no other gods before me," corresponds most closely with what Jesus called the first great commandment: "You will love the Lord your God with all your heart, and with all your soul, and with all your mind, and with all your strength." Just so, the Tenth Commandment or Promise, "You will not covet . . . anything that is your neighbor's," corresponds most closely with what Jesus called the second great commandment: "You will love your neighbor as yourself." It is indeed the key to the whole second table of the law. If God frees our hearts from covetousness and gives us contentment, we will have no need to neglect aging parents, to kill, to commit adultery, to steal, to bear false witness.

Some of my friends think it is foolish to be writing about the Ten Commandments when the threat of nuclear holocaust still hangs over our planet, when the hands of the doomsday clock are still only a few minutes before midnight. The quest for peace is terribly complex and needs to be worked out on many levels. But if covetousness, as we have said, is one of the main destroyers of peace on all levels, then the absolutely essential starting point for peace is love of neighbor—not a vague, undefined love that evaporates in kindly feelings, but a love that refuses to covet what the neighbor has, that works tirelessly for the neighbor's good and advantage.

God's dream is of a world where people are more concerned with their neighbors' *good* than with their neighbors' *goods*. Bring your dream to reality, O God, beginning with us. "Let there be peace on earth, and let it begin with me."

Notes

Part One: The Lord's Prayer

1. Ernest F. Scott, *The Lord's Prayer* (New York: Charles Scribner's Sons, 1951), p. 73.

2. Donald W. Shriver, Jr., *The Lord's Prayer: A Way of Life* (Atlanta: John Knox Press, 1983), p. 5.

3. George A. Buttrick, *So We Believe, So We Pray* (Nashville: Abingdon-Cokesbury Press, 1951), pp. 133, 140.

4. These problems are also discussed in chapters 11 and 31.

5. Diane Tennis, *Is God the Only Reliable Father?* (Philadelphia: Westminster Press, 1985).

6. Cited in Leonardo Boff, *The Lord's Prayer: The Prayer of Integral Liberation* (Maryknoll, N.Y.: Orbis Books, 1983), p. 39.

7. Emil Brunner, *The Christian Doctrine of God* (London: Lutterworth Press, 1949), pp. 128–132.

8. Martin Buber, *I and Thou* (many editions, beginning in 1924; 2nd English ed., Edinburgh: T. & T. Clark, 1959).

9. Boff, *The Lord's Prayer*, p. 45.

10. For the full text see *Great Shorter Works of Pascal*, tr. Emile Cailliet and John Blankenagel (Philadelphia: Westminster Press, 1948), p. 117.

11. Boff, *The Lord's Prayer*, p. 54.

12. John Bright, *The Kingdom of God* (Nashville: Abingdon-Cokesbury Press, 1953).

13. Shriver, *The Lord's Prayer*, p. 39.

14. Boff, *The Lord's Prayer*, p. 60.

15. John Shelby Spong, *Honest Prayer* (New York: Seabury Press, 1973), p. 61.

16. John Milton, "On His Blindness."

17. Confessions cited may be found in *The Constitution of the Presbyterian Church (U.S.A.), Part I: Book of Confessions* (New York and Atlanta: Office of the General Assembly, 1983).

18. "A Declaration of Faith" is a document recommended for study and liturgy by the General Assembly of the Presbyterian Church, U.S., in 1977. This citation is from ch. 2, sec. 1, lines 14–15.

19. Buttrick, *So We Believe, So We Pray,* pp. 176–179.

20. Boff, *The Lord's Prayer,* p. 76.

21. From the hymn "What a Friend We Have in Jesus" by Joseph Scriven, c. 1855.

22. J. D. Jones, *The Model Prayer* (New York: George H. Doran Co.), 1899.

23. "Give Us This Day Our Daily Bread" by Maltbie D. Babcock.

24. Boff, *The Lord's Prayer,* p. 78.

25. Boff, *The Lord's Prayer,* p. 90.

26. "A Declaration of Faith," ch. 4, sec. 4, lines 96–98.

27. Shriver, *The Lord's Prayer,* p. 75.

28. Compare the discussion of this same point in chapter 24.

29. Shriver, *The Lord's Prayer,* p. 72.

30. From the hymn "How Firm a Foundation," 1787.

31. From the hymn "In the Hour of Trial" by James Montgomery, 1834.

32. See the *Didache* 8:2.

33. Boff, *The Lord's Prayer,* pp. 97, 109.

34. Shriver, *The Lord's Prayer,* p. 91.

35. Shriver, *The Lord's Prayer,* p. 92.

Part Two: The Apostles' Creed

1. Rachel Henderlite, *A Call to Faith* (Richmond: John Knox Press, 1955), p. 12.

2. Søren Kierkegaard, *Training in Christianity* (Princeton, N.J.: Princeton University Press, 1947), pp. 79–144.

3. Blaise Pascal, *Pensées,* no. 233.

4. Robert Browning, "Bishop Blougram's Apology," lines 627, 629.

5. These problems are also discussed in chapters 2 and 31.

6. Diane Tennis, *Is God the Only Reliable Father?* (Philadelphia: Westminster Press, 1985), p. 34.

7. See Karl Barth, *Church Dogmatics* II/2, §33.

8. "A Declaration of Faith," ch. 4, sec. 5, lines 135–150; cited in Part One, note 18.

9. I am indebted to Hendrikus Berkhof for this understanding of "the double relation between the Spirit and Christ." See his *The Doctrine of the Holy Spirit* (Richmond: John Knox Press, 1964), pp. 17–21.

10. William Cowper, "Light Shining Out of Darkness," adapted for inclusivity.

11. From the hymn "Lo, How a Rose E'er Blooming," tr. Theodore Baker, 1894; adapted for inclusivity.

12. *Macbeth*, act II, scene 2, lines 61–64.

13. John Donne, *Devotions* 12.

14. From the hymn "There Is a Green Hill Far Away" by Cecil F. Alexander, 1848.

15. "A Declaration of Faith," ch. 10, sec. 3, lines 33–36, 39–40, 42, 47–48, 51–54.

16. James Smart, *The Creed in Christian Teaching* (Philadelphia: Westminster Press, 1962), p. 159.

17. "A Declaration of Faith," ch. 4, sec. 5, lines 131–134.

18. Robert Browning, "Saul," stanza 18.

19. "A Declaration of Faith," ch. 10, sec. 2, lines 14, 23–31.

20. Karl Barth, *Dogmatics in Outline*, tr. G. T. Thomson (New York: Philosophical Library, 1949), p. 143.

21. C. S. Lewis, *The Screwtape Letters* (New York: Macmillan Co., 1961 ed.), p. 12.

22. From the hymn "The Day Thou Gavest, Lord, Is Ended" by John Ellerton, 1870.

23. Compare the discussion of forgiveness in chapter 7.

24. H. Wheeler Robinson, *The Old Testament: Its Making and Meaning* (Nashville: Cokesbury Press, 1937), p. 83.

25. Oswald McCall, *The Hand of God* (New York: Harper & Brothers, 1957), p. 123.

26. From the hymn "Blest Be the Tie That Binds" by John Fawcett, 1782.

Part Three: The Ten Commandments

1. For a clear table illustrating this, see Walter Harrelson, *The Ten Commandments and Human Rights* (Philadelphia: Fortress Press, 1980), p. 47.

2. Harrelson disagrees (p. 48). He suggests that the two tables may mean two copies of a single table and proposes a fourfold division.

3. See Martin Luther, *Commentary on Galatians,* on 3:19 and 4:3.

4. I am indebted to an unpublished manuscript of Markus Barth for the intriguing suggestion that the Ten Words are priestly rubrics like so much else in Exodus.

5. Jan Lochman, *Signposts to Freedom* (Minneapolis: Augsburg Press, 1982), p. 21.

6. Gerhard von Rad, *Old Testament Theology* (New York: Harper & Brothers), vol. I, pp. 194–195.

7. See Andrew Greeley, *The Sinai Myth* (Garden City, N.Y.: Doubleday & Co., 1972), p. 61.

8. Lochman, *Signposts to Freedom,* pp. 13–20.

9. Harrelson, *Ten Commandments,* p. 13.

10. In the Foreword to Harrelson, *Ten Commandments,* p. xiii.

11. Bruce Larson, *The Presence: the God Who Delivers and Guides* (San Francisco: Harper & Row, 1988), p. 72.

12. See Harrelson, *Ten Commandments,* p. 42.

13. Paul Tillich, *Systematic Theology,* part 2, ch. 9, "The Meaning of God."

14. H. H. Farmer, *The World and God* (London: William Collins & Sons, 1963), p. 29 and throughout.

15. H. Richard Niebuhr, *Radical Monotheism and Western Culture* (New York: Harper & Row, 1970), ch. 1.

16. The opening sentence of the Scots Confession, 1560.

17. "A Declaration of Faith," ch. 1, sec. 6, lines 40–43; cited in Part One, note 18.

18. John Calvin, *Institutes of the Christian Religion* (Philadelphia: Westminster Press, 1960), I.11.9.

19. Calvin, *Institutes* I.5.12.

20. Greeley, *Sinai Myth,* p. 111.

21. Tillich makes this point again and again in his *Systematic Theology.*

22. Greeley, *Sinai Myth,* p. 114.

23. Harrelson, *The Ten Commandments,* p. 72.

24. Calvin, *Institutes* II.8.22.

25. At this point the reader may wish to review the discussion of God's name in chapter 3 of this book.

26. John Woolman, *The Journal of John Woolman* (Secaucus, N.J.: Citadel Press, 1975), pp. 214–215.

27. "I Know a Name," author unknown.

28. Tilden Edwards, *Spiritual Friend* (New York: Paulist Press, 1980), p. 69.

29. Some may be surprised to learn that John Calvin was of this opinion. See his *Institutes* II.8.28–34.

30. Charles E. Hambrick-Stowe, *The Practice of Piety: Puritan Devotional Disciplines in Seventeenth-Century New England* (Chapel Hill, N.C.: University of North Carolina Press, 1982).

31. Hambrick-Stowe, pp. xv–xvi.

32. Edwards, *Spiritual Friend,* pp. 69–89. Edwards went on to write a whole book on the subject, *Sabbath Time* (New York: Seabury Press, 1982).

33. Cited in *Spiritual Friend,* pp. 77–82.

34. Karl Barth, *Church Dogmatics* (Edinburgh: T. & T. Clark, 1961), III/4, pp. 47–72.

35. Lochman, *Signposts of Freedom,* pp. 57–63.

36. See the discussion in Harrelson, *Ten Commandments,* pp. 93–94; compare Exodus 21:17.

37. Lochman, *Signposts to Freedom* pp. 79, 82.

38. Calvin, *Institutes* II.8.35, 38.

39. Lochman, *Signposts to Freedom,* p. 80.

40. Greeley, *Sinai Myth,* p. 147.

41. Calvin, *Institutes* II.8.39.

42. Harrelson, *Ten Commandments,* 1980, p. 110.

43. Barth, *Church Dogmatics,* III/4, pp. 397–470.

44. "A Declaration of Faith," ch. 2, sec. 5, lines 84–91.

45. A point made forcibly by Lochman in *Signposts to Freedom,* pp. 125–132.

46. Calvin, *Institutes* II.8.45.

47. *The Journal of John Woolman* (Secaucus, N.J.: Citadel Press, 1975), p. 18.

48. Calvin, *Institutes* II.8.49–50.